ESL/ELL TEACHER'S GUIDE

PACEMAKER®

United States History

Fourth Edition

GLOBE FEARON

Pearson Learning Group

Reviewers

Sheila D. Acevedo, ESOL Manager for Alternative Education,
Palm Beach School District, Palm Beach, FL

Ann Hilborn, former ESL/ELL teacher, coordinator, and curriculum writer for the
Houston Independent School District; currently an ESL/ELL consultant in Texas

Barbara Ishida, Bilingual Language Development Specialist,
Modesto City Schools, Modesto, CA

Linda D. Larson, ESOL Resource Teacher/Coordinator,
School Board of Palm Beach County, Royal Palm Beach, FL

Maribel Nieves, ESL/ELL Teacher, Martin Luther King, Jr. High School, New York, NY

Sandra Prez, Bilingual Coordinator, District 116, Round Lake, IL

Joseph Sklar, Instructional Facilitator, Oakland Unified School District, Oakland, CA

The following people have contributed to the development of this product:

Art & Design: Patricia Battipede, Evelyn Bauer, Susan Brorein, Jenifer Hixson, Angel Weyant
Editorial: Elaine Fay, Jane Petlinski, Jennie Rakos
Manufacturing: Mark Cirillo
Marketing: Katie Erezuma
Production: Irene Belinsky, Karen Edmonds, Suellen Leavy, Jennifer Murphy
Publishing Operations: Travis Bailey, Thomas Daning, Kate Matracia

All photography © Pearson Education, Inc. (PEI) unless otherwise specifically noted.

Cover: *Space Shuttle* NASA; *Flag* Gallery of the Republic; *Pottery* © Phil Shermeister/Corbis;
Train © Bettmann/Corbis.

ISBN 0-13-024423-6
Printed in the United States of America
  2 3 4 5 6 7 8 9 10   07 06 05 04

1-800-321-3106
www.pearsonlearning.com

Contents

Teaching ESL/ELL in the Classroom

As cross-cultural mobility increases, teachers are mindful of their responsibility in the preparation of global citizens. All classrooms are becoming ESL/ELL classrooms, and many teachers are confronting new instructional challenges as demographics shift and diversity multiplies.

On the one hand, there is concern for meeting the needs of students who bring issues and challenges that teachers often feel underprepared to meet. On the other, there is renewal and excitement as teachers and students open to the perspectives of other cultures, and classrooms assume an international orientation.

Helping the ESL/ELL learner to succeed in the academic classroom has required all educators to rethink their roles as teacher, to search for new instructional tools, and to become simultaneously a language teacher, reading teacher, and academic content teacher. To help teachers meet this formidable task, both students and teachers must have teaching and learning resources that make academic content accessible.

The Pacemaker® Curriculum

Typically, schools adopt one of two structures for academic classes: sheltered content or regular mainstream. The Pacemaker® curriculum is perfectly suited for either of those environments. Designed for students who read independently at a 3.0 to 4.0 reading level, a Pacemaker® text normally corresponds to a student at mid-intermediate level of language proficiency. This is the level when most ESL/ELL students are required to deal with the cognitively demanding language of academic content classes.

When students are given sheltered content instruction, the Pacemaker® curriculum is an ideal classroom text for intermediate and advanced level students.

Because the Pacemaker® materials are within the expected reading levels of a second-language learner and the content is presented in manageable sections, ESL/ELL students are encouraged and enabled to be active participants rather than silent observers in the academic classroom.

In schools where sheltered content classes are unavailable, Pacemaker® can be a valuable text or resource for ESL/ELL students in the regular content classroom because it provides information in small manageable sections at a level that students can comprehend.

When Pacemaker® materials are provided in place of, or in addition to, the standard text, students can access academic content rather than struggle with a grade-level text that is beyond their current language proficiency. Although language skills of ESL/ELL students are in a developmental stage, they can be held to the same high standards of critical inquiry as their on-level classmates when input is comprehensible. The Pacemaker® curriculum is also an ideal tool that can be used to preview and review by preparing students for and enhancing their comprehension of the content they will be accessing in their grade-level tests.

How Do I Use the *Pacemaker® ESL/ELL Guide* in My Classroom?

Teaching academic content requires attention to both information and skills. While content teachers are not reading teachers, time spent previewing and engaging in prestudy activities provides an opportunity to teach valuable skills that will serve students in all areas of studies. For ESL/ELL students, time spent in previewing will assure greater comprehension and retention. It will prepare them not only for reading, but also for participation in class discussions, collaborative work, and individual or group projects.

The following suggestions are easily managed in a sheltered content class. If the class is a regular-content class, ESL/ELL students can be provided with a Pacemaker® text while others use a grade-level text. If an aide is not available to work with ESL/ELL students and the teacher must work with both groups, it is not necessary to divide the class and teach two separate groups. Using the high-interest Pacemaker® texts for ESL/ELL students makes it possible to integrate two different texts under unifying objectives. The abundance of resources in the Pacemaker® curriculum to support instruction makes it possible to provide alternate materials with minimum effort.

Each chapter of the Pacemaker® Student Edition is supported by a two-page lesson plan, which follows an Into-Through-Beyond model. The lesson plan begins by introducing students to the chapter content, or bringing them into the content. It then helps students work through the content they have acquired by engaging in relevant activities. Finally, it takes students beyond what they have learned by assessing what they learned and affording them an opportunity to summarize the important points of the chapter.

Introducing the Chapter

This section is made up of two parts: Tapping Prior Knowledge and Preteaching Vocabulary.

Tapping Prior Knowledge

All students, and ESL/ELL students in particular, improve comprehension when they can connect what they already know to the subject. Focusing on the colorful artwork, the title, a caption, a subheading, or a Pacemaker® feature will help students to make important initial connections.

Tapping Prior Knowledge gives students the opportunity to

- preview the chapter.
- access their prior knowledge about a topic.
- think about an overarching question that connects students prior knowledge to chapter content.

Preteaching Vocabulary

Preteaching Vocabulary offers students an opportunity to:

- identify and define words and phrases that are unfamiliar to them. You may wish to ask students to keep a Word Log in which they can list the words and phrases that they identify for Personalizing Vocabulary. This is also an opportunity for students to learn the proper pronunciation of the vocabulary words and phrases. When reviewing the pronunciation of the vocabulary words and phrases with your students, you may wish to pronounce them and have students listen to the pronunciation; pronounce them and ask your students to repeat each one; or pronounce them and have your students repeat them in a choral read. You may wish to provide a phonetic spelling for students to use in addition to the strategies mentioned above.

- engage in a variety of activities across chapters that are based on specific, academic content words and phrases that are integral to their understanding of the subject matter, as well as words and phrases that are challenging for ESL/ELL students, such as double-meaning words and phrases and idiomatic expressions.

Learning Objectives

All learners need concrete and concise explanations of what they will be expected to learn. Every Pacemaker® outlines specific Learning Objectives for each chapter. Reading those objectives with your students as they begin the chapter connects them all to the same goals, guides the lesson, and helps prepare students for future assessment.

Turn to the end of the chapter and have students work in pairs or small groups to connect Learning Objectives to the Chapter Review. Good students use questions in the text to guide them in reading and understanding. ESL/ELL students need to be directed to these tools and shown how the tools can help them to understand what they are reading and studying. This will reinforce what students are expected to learn and help to guide their reading. You may also wish to distribute the Chapter Goals and Self-assessment on page 84 of this guide and have students write the list of objectives that they are expected to master by the end of the chapter. This will allow students to evaluate their own achievement of learning goals.

Applying Content Knowledge

All students improve comprehension when they are able to apply what they have learned. Activities that incorporate the use of graphic organizers as well as activities that allow students to (re)address chapter content help cultivate the initial connections they made in Tapping Prior Knowledge.

Each activity in Applying Content Knowledge:

- uses Specifically Designed Academic Instruction in English strategies. SDAIE strategies focus on delivering grade-level content and covering grade-level standards in a way that is personally relevant for and comprehensible to the student.

- uses the Cognitive Academic Language Learning Approach. CALLA is designed to help ESL/ELL students succeed academically by addressing topics from the major content subjects, developing academic language skills, and offering explicit instruction on learning strategies.
- offers activities that enhance students' content knowledge through reading, writing, speaking, and listening.
- allows students to use a variety of graphic organizers. Several organizers are provided on pages 48–68 of this guide. Using them will not only help students to understand what they read, it will also teach them the variety of ways material is organized.

Assessing Content Knowledge

This section provides three levels of questions tailored to beginning ESL/ELL students, intermediate ESL/ELL students, and advanced ESL/ELL students. [See page viii of this guide for placement criteria.] Questions can be answered orally or in writing. This section also provides teachers' annotations at point of use.

As an alternative, the leveled questions can also be used for discussion. If the questions are used for discussion, allow ESL/ELL students adequate time to process the question by using a cooperative strategy like putting students in small groups made up of students with varied language abilities. Pose the question and then allow the group to process the answer so that each group member can respond. Then, allow one member of each group to give an answer. This strategy is also ideal for reviewing chapter content.

Beginning Level Students

- Specific page references are provided to scaffold beginning ESL/ELL students.
- Beginning ESL/ELL students are asked to respond to questions using short verbal responses.

Intermediate Level Students

- More general skill or section references are provided to scaffold intermediate ESL/ELL students.
- Intermediate ESL/ELL students are asked to respond to questions using verbal responses or short written responses.

Advanced Level Students

- Since advanced students are expected to be able to answer the questions in the Chapter Review at the end of each chapter in the Student Edition, no page or skill/section references are provided for the advanced ESL/ELL students.
- Advanced ESL/ELL students are asked to respond to questions in complete written sentences.

Closing the Chapter

Closing the Chapter provides an opportunity for students to assess the key points of the chapter and summarize them. Students are frequently asked to write a summary about what they learned, but you may wish to ask beginning ESL/ELL students to give an oral report of what they learned.

Selecting the Appropriate Leveled Questions

This guide includes three levels of questions to address the different levels of students' language proficiency.

Since there are students who can speak English but have difficulty reading it, the leveled questions presented in this guide should be chosen for a student based on the student's level of reading proficiency. The following criteria are based on student competencies at the beginning of the year, which are expected to increase during the course of the academic year. The three levels of questions provided in each lesson plan of this guide are also available as reproducible pages that can be downloaded from www.esl-ell.com. Level A corresponds to the Beginning Level Questions; Level B corresponds to the Intermediate Level Questions; and Level C corresponds to the Advanced Level Questions.

▶ Beginning Level Questions – Level A

Beginning Level Students:
- range from having no comprehension to the ability to read and comprehend simple sentences in present continuous or simple present tense.
- are able to answer straightforward comprehension questions (*who, what, when, where*) that require only simple responses.
- are able to write paragraphs of one to five lines.
- are able to read and write at a kindergarten to a first-grade level.
- should be able to complete the Beginning Level Questions in this guide.

▶ Intermediate Level Questions – Level B

Intermediate Level Students:
- satisfy all of the beginning level criteria.
- are able to read and comprehend simple past and future tense sentences.
- are able to answer comprehension questions that also include *how* and *why* with more complex responses.
- are able to write a well-developed paragraph.
- are able to read and write from a second- to a fourth-grade level.
- should be able to complete the Intermediate Level Questions in this guide.

▶ Advanced Level Questions – Level C

Advanced Level Students:
- satisfy all of the beginning and intermediate level criteria.
- are able to read and comprehend more complex sentence constructions.
- are able to use past and some perfect tense constructions in their writing.
- are able to respond to questions that require inference and conclusions.
- are able to write multi-paragraph compositions.
- are able to read and write at a level that can extend from third to fifth grade.
- should be able to complete the questions in the Chapter Review in the Student Edition as well as the Advanced Level Questions in this guide.

Effective Strategies for ESL/ELL Students

While the *Pacemaker® ESL/ELL Guide* is designed to help teachers of ESL/ELL students help their students access content knowledge, there are some additional strategies that are centered around the motivation of and effective study skills for ESL/ELL students.

Classroom Techniques

Encourage risk-taking by keeping a low-anxiety environment.

- Strive for genuine communication with students. Students' fears are calmed when teachers share information about themselves and invite students to talk about themselves and their experiences.
- Provide game-like activities.
- Adjust speech. Speak a little more slowly and distinctly.
- Share information across cultures.
- Provide materials that support comprehension.
- Practice a little of the students' languages.

Provide academic scaffolds to help your students access the content.

- Model all activities for your students. Provide examples and writing models.
- Give students a topic outline for note-taking.
- Encourage students to use previewing strategies, while-reading strategies, and post-reading strategies.
- Provide study questions and guides.
- Identify organizational cues, such as titles, subtitles, and charts.
- Afford students longer reading time, as well as extended time for assignments and test completion.

Building Language Skills

Read to students. By reading short passages in answer to a question or as an introduction, ESL/ELL students receive the added benefit of hearing academic language, cadence, rhythm, and pronunciation.

When reading from a source other than the Student Edition, provide handouts or use an overhead, so students can see and hear the information.

Teach students to read academic material several times. As academic learners, we all expect to read a selection, a page, a chapter, or a section more than once. Encourage students to:

- survey an academic assignment once for general information and vocabulary.
- organize reading into smaller chunks for understanding.
- read a third time for higher-level critical thinking skills.

In-class reading time is usually no more than 10 to 15 minutes. Regular classroom students may be expected to read more material in that time frame, but they need not read for a longer period of time. If longer reading assignments are desired for homework, reading can be previewed in advance of any assignment and graphic organizers provided to help guide ESL/ELL students' reading.

Maximize language output. While students should be given opportunities to interact without depending heavily on language, the more practical opportunities students have to speak and write, the more proficient they will become. These opportunities may begin with communication of their own life experiences and world knowledge.

Provide open-ended writing assignments and opportunities for ESL/ELL students to express their thoughts and feelings. Some of these include:

- journals.
- descriptions of experiences or feelings.
- response to art, photos, and audio-visuals.

The Tapping Prior Knowledge section, which highlights the art and photos in each chapter and often asks students to relate the content to their own experiences, is an ideal opportunity for students to express their thoughts and feelings. For example, you may wish to ask students to keep a journal and record their initial responses to the visual image(s) that appear(s) on the first page of each chapter. You may also consider having students choose to describe a visual image that appears in the chapter.

Complete activities with a writing assignment. ESL/ELL students may need adjustments to the writing assignments, such as:

- shorter writing assignments.
- more time to complete writing.
- frequent opportunities to work with peers in revising and editing.

Occasionally it will be necessary to assign a different topic. *The Pacemaker® ESL/ELL Guide* provides writing opportunities in conjunction with many of the activities that help students reinforce chapter content.

Learning Strategies

Provide opportunities for different groups to work together, share information, and be a resource for each other.

Provide opportunities for students to interact without depending heavily on language. Students can work to access content knowledge by:

- doing projects and making posters, pictures, and collages.
- using manipulatives.
- using charts.
- using numbered lists, bulleted lists, graphs, tables, and models.
- role-playing.

Use visuals, pictures, realia, video clips, and actions to teach vocabulary and to make concepts concrete and understandable. Maps, play money, artwork, globes, and pictures are effective, tangible ways to help students access content.

Use graphic organizers for note-taking, organizing information, and writing. Diagrams and charts are an effective way to teach students to organize information and visualize patterns and structures. Graphic organizers can be downloaded from www.esl-ell.com.

Customizing Student Assessment

Assess your students' successes by focusing on the "big picture."

- Grade a combination of process and product.
- Recognize effort and improvement in ways other than grades.
- Allow rewrites and test corrections to improve grades and understanding.
- Congratulate students on small successes.
- Focus on meaning and content knowledge, not grammar mistakes, in students' written work.
- Use alternative assessments, such as performance-based assessments, self-ratings, projects, and portfolios.
- Adjust your grading scale where appropriate.

At Home

Help students manage their own success. Reinforce the importance of organizing homework, academic tasks, and extracurricular activities using a calendar like the one shown below.

Monday	Tuesday	Wednesday	Thursday	Friday
soccer practice 3:00-5:30	study time 5:00-6:00	soccer practice 3:00-5:30	study time 5:00-6:00	
dinner 6:00-7:00	dinner 6:00-7:00	dinner 6:00-7:00	dinner 6:00-7:00	dinner 6:00-7:00
study time 7:00-8:00	orchestra 7:30-9:00		climbing club 8:00-9:00	

You may wish to work with students to schedule activities from this guide that you assign as homework. Homework gives parents and caregivers an opportunity to be involved with their students.

Ann Hilborn

Ann Hilborn, a former ESL/ELL teacher, coordinator, and curriculum writer for the Houston Independent School District, is currently an ESL/ELL consultant in Texas.

Previewing Strategies

When students preview, they set a purpose for reading, they think about what they already know about a topic, and they get a general idea of what they will learn. Activities that students engage in before reading help them prepare to learn new information. Previewing helps students incorporate what they read into their existing knowledge. During previewing, students should identify key terms, assess the level of difficulty and length of what they will be reading, gain a general sense of the topic and major subtopics, understand text organization, and determine how this information relates to what they already know.

Create a Plan for Reading.

This task requires students to think about why they are reading. *What was the purpose of the assignment?* If students are unclear about the answer to this question, they need to find out why they are reading. Next, students should look at the assignment to get a sense of how difficult it is. *Can they read the assignment in one session, or should they break it into several sessions?*

Think About What They Know About the Topic.

Students who engage with the text create a scaffold for learning. When they bring prior knowledge to bear on their readings, students become involved with the text.

Preview the Selection.

When students preview, they think about what they already know about a topic and get a general idea of what they will learn. Students should:

- look at the title and subheadings. These signal important ideas and usually hint at text organization.
- look at other visual aids. These include words within the text in italic or bold type, which may be vocabulary words or new concepts. Students should also look at aids, such as maps, photos, charts, illustrations, numbered lists, and bulleted lists. This will give ESL/ELL students more contextual information to aid with comprehension.
- read the first and last paragraphs. These often contain the thesis or major points of the reading. Remind students to connect what they are previewing with what they already know about the topic.
- read the first sentence or topic sentence of each paragraph. Often, the main point of a paragraph is found at the beginning.
- get an idea of the text structure. If students understand how the text is organized—for example, chronologically or in cause-and-effect form—they will be better able to follow the text.

Vocabulary Strategies

Each two-page lesson plan provides a vocabulary activity for its chapter. While the vocabulary activities in this guide support the chapters they are featured in, they can also be used for any other chapter in the book. In addition to the specific vocabulary activities offered in this guide, following are some general vocabulary strategies to consider when teaching new vocabulary to students.

▶ Create Word Logs.

Students should be encouraged to keep Word Logs that they can use to record the vocabulary they identify for the Personalizing Vocabulary activity of the two-page lesson plan in this guide. The Word Log can be a spiral notebook divided by letters of the alphabet with a second section for phrases. Students can write definitions, sentences, or draw or cut out from magazines pictures to aid them in understanding and remembering.

▶ Pronounce Vocabulary Words and Phrases.

It is critical to pronounce vocabulary words and phrases for ESL/ELL students. As in the case of reading to your students, pronouncing new words and phrases allows students to grow accustomed to cadence and rhythm. When reviewing the pronunciation of the vocabulary words and phrases, you may wish to:

- pronounce each word and phrase for your students and have them listen to the pronunciation.
- pronounce each word and phrase for your students and ask your students to repeat each one.
- pronounce each word and phrase for your students and then have your students repeat them all in a choral read.
- provide a phonetic spelling for students to use in addition to the strategies mentioned above.

▶ Think About the Topic.

Help students make a connection between the new vocabulary word or phrase and a word or phrase in their own language. This allows them to see the word or phrase in their native language and aids in retention. Suggest also that ESL/ELL students refer to their first language for cognates or similar words.

▶ Monitor Comprehension.

Students have several opportunities to learn the academic vocabulary that appears in the Student Edition. However, students are not always comfortable or familiar with all of the words and phrases used in daily conversation, such as idiomatic expressions and colloquialisms. Always ask students if they understand the words and phrases that you use during the course of your lesson delivery. Your inquiry can be after a few sentences or after the use of a word or expression that you are unsure your students understand, but it should be frequent.

▷ Introducing the Chapter

Tapping Prior Knowledge

Ask students to preview the chapter by reading the headings and subheadings and by looking at the art and photos (on pages 1, 2, 6, 11, and 16 of the Student Edition), the timelines (on pages 2–3 and 10 of the Student Edition), the maps (on pages 5, 8, 12, and 14 of the Student Edition), the numbered lists (on pages 8 and 9 of the Student Edition), and the chart (on page 15 of the Student Edition). Then, ask students to study the heading entitled *Groups Live in Different Ways* on page 7 of the Student Edition. Ask students, *How might a group that moves from one place to another adapt traditions to suit its new environment?*

Preteaching Vocabulary

Personalizing Vocabulary Begin by asking students to preview the chapter for five unfamiliar words or phrases and to record them in their Word Logs. Once students have identified these words and phrases, ask them to use their dictionaries to define them.

Identifying Essential Vocabulary Go over the pronunciation and meaning of each word and phrase in the box below. Then, ask students to work in pairs and write three sentences for each word and phrase in the box below. You may wish to begin by writing a sentence on the chalkboard for each word and each phrase that students can model.

Word or Phrase	Meaning
may have reached	might have arrived (p.3)
trapped	caught (p.4)
gathered	collected (p.6)
crops	plants like grains, vegetables, and fruit (p.6)
shelter	protection from the weather (p.6)
besides	in addition to (p.6)
suited to	appropriate for (p.7)
scarce	limited (p.11)
turned away	to send from a place (p.16)

▷ Applying Content Knowledge

From the Chapter: History and You (page 16)

Ask students to read History and You: The Columbian Exchange on page 16 of the Student Edition. Ask students to make a list of foods from the country that they or their family originally came from. Then, ask students to draw or cut from magazines pictures of the foods, paste them onto chart paper, and name the country and continent the foods come from. Under each picture, ask students to write a sentence for each food using the following model: Coffee comes from Colombia, South America.

Organizing Information

Distribute the two-column chart on page 68 of this guide. Ask students to write the heading **Positive Things About Early Exploration** at the top of the first column and the heading **Negative Things About Early Exploration** at the top of the second column. Then, have students list the positive and negative things about early exploration and decide if the exploration was positive or negative. You may wish to ask students to write a paragraph to explain their choice.

Using Visuals

Distribute copies of the World Map on page 69 of this guide. Ask students to label the continents. Then, ask students to add the names of the ancient civilizations in North America, South America, and Africa. You may also wish to ask students to identify their continent/country.

Personalizing the Lesson

Ask students to choose one civilization from the Incas, Mayas, and Aztecs and write a paragraph from the point of view of someone who lived during that time. Students' paragraphs might address the following questions: *Where did he/she live? When? What kind of shelter, food, and clothing did he/she have? Did he/she work? Could he/she read, write, and/or do mathematics? Was he/she rich or poor?*

Assessing Content Knowledge

Ask students to respond to the following questions. You may wish to encourage students with higher language proficiency to help beginning level students understand the questions.

Beginning Level Questions

Encourage students at this level to think about the answers to these questions and offer short verbal responses.

1. Look at the map on page 5. What three continents are shown? (Asia, North America, South America)

2. Look at pages 8–9. What are the four civilizations? (Olmecs, Mayas, Incas, and Aztecs)

3. Look at the old map on page 12. List four things you see. (Answers will vary. Possible answers include men, horses, camels, and soldiers.)

4. Look at the map on page 14. What are the names of the three West African kingdoms? (Ghana, Mali, and Songhai)

5. Look at the chart on page 15. What four explorers are listed in the first column? (John Cabot, Amerigo Vespucci, Vasco Núñez de Balboa, and Ferdinand Magellan)

Intermediate Level Questions

Encourage students at this level to offer verbal responses or short written responses to the following questions.

1. Look at Section 1. How did the nomads come to the Americas? (on a land bridge made from glaciers)

2. Look at Section 1. What were five accomplishments of the Mayan civilization? (planted crops; dug ditches to carry water to the fields; formed cities and began trading goods; built large temples and stone courtyards; used a calendar)

3. Look at Section 2. What Asian products did Marco Polo describe? (spices, silk, jewels, carpets)

4. Look at Section 3. What did European explorers want? (to find a route to Asia for riches and wealth)

5. Look at Section 3. What happened to the Arawaks and other Native Americans after explorers came? (died because of battles, diseases, and enslavement)

Advanced Level Questions

Encourage students at this level to provide written responses in complete sentences to the following questions.

1. What is the difference between the way the Native Americans lived in northeastern North America and southwestern North America? (Possible answer: The Native Americans who lived in northeastern North America made shelters of animal skin, bark, or wood. The Native Americans who lived in southwestern North America built shelters from stone and sun-dried clay bricks.)

2. What are two differences between the Olmecs and the Mayans? (Possible answer: The Olmecs developed a number system and a writing system.)

3. What did Marco Polo's adventures do for many European traders? (Marco Polo's adventures may have made many European traders wish to find a shorter way or route to Asia.)

4. What did the three kingdoms that controlled West Africa between 1000 and 1600 have in common? (They were powerful; they had gold; they traded gold for salt; they had slaves.)

5. Why did the Arawaks and thousands of other Native Americans die? (They died from battles with soldiers, European diseases, and enslavement.)

Closing the Chapter

Distribute the Spider Web on page 73 of this guide. Ask students to write **Early America** under the heading **Topic**. Have students write the four most important points they learned from the chapter on the four spokes of the Spider Web. Ask students to use their completed Webs to write a summary about what they learned in the chapter.

Colonies Are Settled (1519–1733)
pages 20–39

▶ Introducing the Chapter

Tapping Prior Knowledge

Ask students to preview the chapter by reading the headings and subheadings and by looking at the art and photos (on pages 20, 22, 23, 26, 28, 29, 31, 33, and 36 of the Student Edition), the timeline (on pages 20–21 of the Student Edition), the numbered lists (on pages 22, 29, and 32 of the Student Edition), the chart (on page 24 of the Student Edition), and the map (on page 35 of the Student Edition). Then, direct students to the paintings on pages 20 and 28 of the Student Edition. Ask students, *What problems or dangers do immigrants have when they come to a new country?*

Preteaching Vocabulary

Personalizing Vocabulary Begin by asking students to preview the chapter for five unfamiliar words or phrases and to record them in their Word Logs. Once students have identified these words and phrases, ask them to use their dictionaries to define them.

Identifying Essential Vocabulary Go over the pronunciation and meaning of each word and phrase in the box below. Then, ask each student to write a sentence for each word. Have students rewrite their sentences, leaving a blank space in place of the vocabulary term. Then, ask students to exchange sentences with a partner and fill in the blanks in the sentences their partner wrote.

Word or Phrase	Meaning
claimed	declared (p.22)
in search of	looking for (p.23)
wildlife	animals and plants that live in nature (p.23)
settler	a person who makes a place his or her home (p.24)
forced	made to do something (p.24)
water route	a path made of water (p.25)
religious beliefs	the way people feel about faith (p.27)
agreement	understanding (p.28)

▶ Applying Content Knowledge

From the Chapter: Connecting History and Science (page 31)

Ask students to read Connecting History and Science: Colonial Medicine on page 31 of the Student Edition. Then, have students work in groups to list the medical cures that today we know were useless or even foolish. Next, have students predict five cures we use today that will probably appear to be foolish 200 years from now. These include radiation, surgery, vaccinations, antibiotics, and chemotherapy. Ask students, *Why do you believe that the cures you listed will be useless or seem foolish 200 years from now?*

Organizing Information

Explain to students that a chart can give essential information in a short form. Ask students to make a five-column chart of the three early English settlements in North America. Ask students to label the columns **Name of the Colony, Date of Settlement, Reason for Settlement, Leader,** and **Problems.** You may wish to distribute the four-column chart on page 70 of this guide and have students draw an additional column.

Personalizing the Lesson

Ask students to work in small groups to make a list of reasons that explain why people came to North America to live during the 1700s. Tell them to also list the dangers or problems involved in such a move. After their lists are complete, ask students to decide which reasons or problems/dangers still apply today and which do not.

4   **Unit 1** • U.S. History

Assessing Content Knowledge

Ask students to respond to the following questions. You may wish to encourage students with higher language proficiency to help beginning level students understand the questions.

Beginning Level Questions

Encourage students at this level to think about the answers to these questions and offer short verbal responses.

1. Look at the chart on page 24. Who are four Spanish explorers? (Juan Ponce de León, Hernán Cortés, Francisco Pizarro, and Francisco de Coronado)

2. Look at the picture on page 26. Who is the person? (John Smith, leader of Jamestown)

3. Look at page 27. Who settled in Plymouth? (the Pilgrims)

4. Look at pages 32–37. How many colonies were there? (13)

5. Look at the map on page 35. What three regions are shown? (New England, Middle, Southern)

Intermediate Level Questions

Encourage students at this level to offer verbal responses or short written responses to the following questions.

1. Look at Section 1. Why did Spain want to conquer, or take over, the Aztecs? (for their gold and silver)

2. Look at Section 1. Why were a small number of Spanish soldiers able to conquer the Aztecs? (The Spanish soldiers used cannons, guns, and swords that were more powerful than the bows, arrows, and spears used by the Aztecs; the Aztecs were frightened by the Spanish soldiers' horses; and many Aztecs died from measles and smallpox.)

3. Look at Section 2. What are three things that the Native Americans showed the Pilgrims? (how to grow corn; where to hunt turkey and deer; and ways to fish for food)

4. Look at Section 2. What group of settlers came to New England in 1628? (the Puritans)

5. Look at Section 3. What are the names of the 13 colonies? (Massachusetts, Rhode Island, Connecticut, New Hampshire, New York, New Jersey, Pennsylvania, Delaware, Virginia, Maryland, North Carolina, South Carolina, and Georgia)

Advanced Level Questions

Encourage students at this level to provide written responses in complete sentences to the following questions.

1. What are three European countries that made settlements in the Americas? (Three European countries that made settlements in the Americas are Great Britain, Spain, and France.)

2. What was the Mayflower Compact? (The Mayflower Compact was an agreement written by the leaders of the Pilgrims that stated that all laws of the new colony would be fair and equal.)

3. How did Native Americans help the colonists? (The Native Americans showed the colonists how to grow corn; where to hunt turkey and deer; and ways to fish for food.)

4. What are four religious groups that were established in the colonies? (The four religious groups that were established in the colonies were the Pilgrims, the Catholics, the Puritans, and the Quakers.)

5. How was the colony of Georgia unusual? (It was settled by debtors.)

Closing the Chapter

Ask students to use the chart they created in the Organizing Information activity on page 4 of this guide to write a paragraph about what they learned in the chapter.

Growth of Colonial Society (1630–1760)
pages 40–57

▶ Introducing the Chapter

Tapping Prior Knowledge

Ask students to preview the chapter by reading the headings and subheadings and by looking at the art and photos (on pages 40, 43, 45, 49, 51, and 53 of the Student Edition), the timeline (on pages 40–41 of the Student Edition), the numbered list (on page 44 of the Student Edition), and the map (on page 46 of the Student Edition). Ask students to share their own personal experiences of change. They might consider events like jobs, moving, schools, births, deaths, and marriages. Ask students if these events changed the way they thought about things. Ask students, *How do you suppose changes in the colonies changed the way people thought?*

Preteaching Vocabulary

Personalizing Vocabulary Begin by asking students to preview the chapter for five unfamiliar words or phrases and to record them in their Word Logs. Once students have identified these words and phrases, ask them to use their dictionaries to define them.

Identifying Essential Vocabulary Go over the pronunciation and meaning of each word and phrase in the box below. Then, distribute an index card to each student. Ask each student to write a question on the index card using one or more of the vocabulary words. Then, have students select a partner to exchange cards with and have each student answer his or her partner's question.

Word or Phrase	Meaning
natural resources	something in nature (like gold, silver, or oil) that a country can use (p.42)
port	a place where ships bring things and take other things (p.43)
right	freedom and advantages all people should have (p.44)
goods	things that are made to be sold (p.46)
arrived	came to a place (p.48)
was established	was started (p.50)

▶ Applying Content Knowledge

From the Chapter: Voices From the Past (page 51)

Ask students to read Voices From the Past: Anna Green Winslow on page 51 of the Student Edition. Ask students to study Anna's diary and list her activities on January 11, February 9, and February 22. Then, suggest that students keep a diary of three days in their week. Ask students to think about the differences between their lives and Anna's and why their lives are different. Ask students to write a paragraph about the differences. You might wish to provide this model as a topic sentence: *My life is very different from Anna Green Winslow's.*

Organizing Information

Ask students to write the chapter and section titles from the chapter on a separate sheet of paper. Then, have students work in groups to predict what each of the sections will be about. Ask each group to write a sentence that states each prediction.

Using Visuals

Ask students to look at the art and photos on pages 40, 43, 45, 49, 51, and 53 of the Student Edition. Have students work in groups to determine what we can learn about life in the colonies from these pictures. Ask students, *What kinds of clothes did the colonists wear? What kinds of houses did they live in?*

Personalizing the Lesson

Ask students to review the information on each region. Then, ask students, *If you were a colonist, where would you want to live?* Have students write a paragraph explaining why they would choose to live in one colony and not another.

Assessing Content Knowledge

Ask students to respond to the following questions. You may wish to encourage students with higher language proficiency to help beginning level students understand the questions.

Beginning Level Questions

Encourage students at this level to think about the answers to these questions and offer short verbal responses.

1. Look at page 43. What were two important crops for the Middle colonies? (wheat and rye)

2. Look at page 44. How many economies did the Southern colonies have? (two)

3. Look at the map on page 46. What is the route? (1) from _____ to _____ (2) from _____ to _____ (3) from _____ to _____ (colonies to Africa, Africa to West Indies, West Indies to colonies)

4. Look at page 49. What three places made up the common? (the church, the meetinghouse, and the school)

5. Look at page 54. What two rights did the colonists want? (political and economic)

Intermediate Level Questions

Encourage students at this level to offer verbal responses or short written responses to the following questions.

1. Look at the timelines on pages 20–21 and 40–41. What are four events that happened in the English colonies between 1620 and 1760? (Answers will vary.)

2. Look at Section 1. What is one important thing in the economy of each region? (Answers will vary.)

3. Look at Section 2. Why did people barter with each other? (There was little money, and bartering was a way to get important items.)

4. Look at Section 3. What did the Great Awakening change ideas about? (religion)

5. Look at Section 3. What did the Enlightenment change ideas about? (reason or thought)

Advanced Level Questions

Encourage students at this level to provide written responses in complete sentences to the following questions.

1. How was the economy different for each region of the colonies? (Answers will vary. See pages 42–44 of the Student Edition.)

2. Why was slavery important to the Southern colonies? (They wanted workers for the large plantations.)

3. What did the leaders of the Enlightenment believe about government? (They believed that the government should protect "lives and liberty and prosperity.")

4. What were two political rights and two economic rights the colonists wanted? (Answers will vary.)

5. Why did the Navigation Acts make the colonists angry? (Colonists had to pay more money for goods that came from other countries because of the taxes.)

Closing the Chapter

Ask students to review the predictions they made in the Organizing Information activity on page 6 of this guide. Have students revise their predictions to reflect what they learned in the chapter. Then, ask students to write a paragraph that summarizes what they learned.

Chapter 4

The Struggle for Freedom (1754–1783)

pages 58–79

▶ Introducing the Chapter

Tapping Prior Knowledge

Ask students to preview the chapter by reading the headings and the subheadings and by looking at the art and photos (on pages 58, 60, 61, 65, 69, 70, 72, 73, 75, and 77 of the Student Edition), the timeline (on pages 58–59 of the Student Edition), the chart (on page 64 of the Student Edition), and the map (on page 74 of the Student Edition). Then, ask students to think about what freedom means to them. Encourage students to share personal thoughts or experiences that relate to the idea of freedom. Then, ask students, *How does this help you to understand the experiences of the colonists and their desire for freedom?*

Preteaching Vocabulary

Personalizing Vocabulary Begin by asking students to preview the chapter for five unfamiliar words or phrases and to record them in their Word Logs. Once students have identified these words and phrases, ask them to use their dictionaries to define them.

Identifying Essential Vocabulary Go over the pronunciation and meaning of each word and phrase in the box below. Then, ask students to look at the word *taxation*. Explain that the word comes in many forms: *tax, taxes, taxable,* and *taxing. Tax* is a noun that means "a fee," and *taxes* is the plural form of *tax; taxable* is an adjective, and *taxing* is a verb. Tell students that it is often possible to find the meaning of a word if you know the meaning of one of its other forms.

Word or Phrase	Meaning
canoe	a light, skinny boat that you move using paddles (p.60)
troop	a military group (p.62)
taxation	the act of making people pay taxes (p.64)
rang out	made a noise (p.65)
overboard	over the side of a boat or ship (p.65)
public meeting	a gathering everyone can attend (p.65)
stand your ground	to hold your position (p.68)

▶ Applying Content Knowledge

From the Chapter: British Acts Against the Colonies (page 64)

Ask students to look at the British Acts Against the Colonies chart on page 64 of the Student Edition. Explain that it lists the acts that the British imposed on the colonies. Tell students that an act is an action that is taken, such as making colonists pay a tax. Explain to students that such acts made the colonists angry. Ask students to work in groups to write a short statement about each act and a sentence explaining why each act made the colonists angry. Students can follow this model: *The Proclamation of 1763 said that colonists are not allowed to settle in the Ohio Valley. This made the colonists angry because ___.* After students complete their statements and have shared their answers, ask them, *Why do you think that these acts were serious enough to lead to a revolution?*

Summarizing

Distribute the Sequence of Events chart on page 71 of this guide. Ask students to work in groups to sequence 6 steps toward the independence of the colonies, beginning with the Proclamation of 1763. Suggest that they use the headings as guides. Possible choices might be: *Protests, Boston Massacre, First Continental Congress, Lexington, Concord, Second Continental Congress, Battle of Bunker Hill, Declare Independence, War, Battle of Yorktown, Treaty of Paris.*

Personalizing the Lesson

Ask students to suppose they live in one of the 13 colonies. Ask them to write a letter to a friend to convince him or her to join in the fight for independence. Tell students to use events in Section 3 to support their reasons. For example, *We defeated the British at Concord* or *The British lost twice as many men at Bunker Hill as the colonists.* You may wish to have student volunteers share their letters with a partner or a small group.

Assessing Content Knowledge

Ask students to respond to the following questions. You may wish to encourage students with higher language proficiency to help beginning level students understand the questions.

Beginning Level Questions

Encourage students at this level to think about the answers to these questions and offer short verbal responses.

1. Look at the timeline on page 58. What happened in 1770? (the Boston Massacre)

2. Look at page 61. Which countries were in the French and Indian War? (France and Great Britain)

3. Look at page 64. Which five British laws made the colonists angry? (the Proclamation of 1763, the Sugar Act, the Stamp Act, the Quartering Tax, the Townshend Act)

4. Look at page 70. Who won the battle of Bunker Hill? (the British)

5. Look at page 71. Who was asked to write the Declaration of Independence? (Thomas Jefferson)

Intermediate Level Questions

Encourage students at this level to offer verbal responses or short written responses to the following questions.

1. Look at Section 1. Why did war break out between France and Great Britain? (Great Britain wanted the land west of the Appalachian Mountains that was claimed by France.)

2. Look at Section 2. Why were the colonists dissatisfied with British rule? (because the British imposed five acts)

3. Look at Section 2. What were three results of the Boston Tea Party? (Public meetings were prohibited; Boston Harbor was closed; and more British soldiers were sent to the city.)

4. Look at Section 2. What did the representatives of the First Continental Congress send to Great Britain? (a declaration, or public statement, that listed all the unfair treatment that the colonists faced)

5. Look at Section 3. Why was Thomas Jefferson asked to write the Declaration of Independence? (to explain why the colonies should be free from British rule)

Advanced Level Questions

Encourage students at this level to provide written responses in complete sentences to the following questions.

1. What was the reason for the French and Indian War? (Both France and Great Britain wanted the Ohio River valley.)

2. What was the purpose of the First Continental Congress? (The purpose of the First Continental Congress was to send a Declaration of American Rights to Great Britain.)

3. What was the purpose of the Second Continental Congress? (The purpose of the Second Continental Congress was to try to avoid war [Olive Branch Petition], but also to prepare for war.)

4. What were four important documents produced by the colonists during this period? (Answers will vary, but might include the Declaration of American Rights to Great Britain, the Olive Branch Petition, *Common Sense*, and the Declaration of Independence.)

5. Name six famous colonists who helped win independence and what each of them did. (Possible answers include George Washington, general; Thomas Jefferson, wrote Declaration of Independence; Paul Revere and William Dawes, warned the colonists of a British attack; Benjamin Franklin, obtained French help; Captain John Parker, fought at Lexington; Thomas Paine, wrote *Common Sense*.)

Closing the Chapter

Ask students to use the Sequence of Events chart they created in the Summarizing activity on page 8 of this guide to write a paragraph about what they learned in the chapter.

Chapter 5
Building a New Government (1780–1800)
pages 82–99

▶ Introducing the Chapter

Tapping Prior Knowledge

Ask students to preview the chapter by reading the headings and subheadings and by looking at the art and photos (on pages 81, 82, 84, 85, and 94 of the Student Edition), the timeline (on pages 82–83 of the Student Edition), the numbered lists (on pages 85 and 95 of the Student Edition), the charts (on pages 87 and 91 of the Student Edition), and the map (on page 95 of the Student Edition). Then, direct students to the Checks and Balances chart on page 91 of the Student Edition. Explain that this chart shows the specific powers held by each part of the government. Ask students, *What happens when we do too much of one thing and not enough of another, or when we have too much of one thing and not enough of another?* Then, ask students, *Why is it important to balance the powers of each part of the government?*

Preteaching Vocabulary

Personalizing Vocabulary Begin by asking students to preview the chapter for five unfamiliar words or phrases and to record them in their Word Logs. Once students have identified these words and phrases, ask them to use their dictionaries to define them.

Identifying Essential Vocabulary Go over the pronunciation and meaning of each word and phrase in the box below. Then, ask students to work in pairs to search the text for each word and phrase below and to create a word-sentence match activity for practice.

Word or Phrase	Meaning
controlled	organized (p.84)
revolt	to go against something (p.85)
debt	money that is owed (p.85)
rebellion	to go against something (p.85)
delegate	representative (p.88)
set up	arrange (p.89)
arose	came up (p.90)
repair the damage	fix what is broken (p.93)

▶ Applying Content Knowledge

From the Chapter: Checks and Balances (page 91)

Ask students to look at the Checks and Balances chart on page 91 of the Student Edition. Then, ask students to choose either home, school, or work and to think about how each legislative branch applies to the situation they chose. For example, if students chose home, ask students, *Who sees that laws are enforced at home? Who passes the laws at home?* and *Who interprets the laws at home?*

Using Visuals

Ask students to study the timeline on pages 82–83 of the Student Edition. Then, distribute the Timeline on page 72 of this guide, and ask students to suppose that they were born in 1780. The first 20 years of their lives are on the timeline. Have them work individually to match each event to their age. For example, when the student was age one, the Articles of Confederation were ratified. Then, have students use their personal timeline/events to write an autobiographical paragraph about their lives during that time period.

Personalizing the Lesson

Ask students to read the section entitled Political Parties on page 96 of the Student Edition. Then, distribute the two-column chart on page 68 of this guide and ask students to label the columns **Federalist** and **Democratic-Republic.** Have students list Hamilton's beliefs in the first column and Jefferson's beliefs in the second column. Ask students to decide which party they agree with and then write a paragraph explaining their positions. Remind students that supporting a position requires that they include their reasons. You might also wish to suggest that they illustrate their reasons with examples from life today.

Assessing Content Knowledge

Ask students to respond to the following questions. You may wish to encourage students with higher language proficiency to help beginning level students understand the questions.

Beginning Level Questions

Encourage students at this level to think about the answers to these questions and offer short verbal responses.

1. Look at the timeline on pages 82–83. When was the Articles of Confederation ratified? (1781)

2. Look at page 85. What are four problems that the United States faced after the war? (The United States had to find new trading partners; debts could not be paid; money from one state was worthless in another state; and there were no courts to settle arguments between states.)

3. Look at page 90. What are the three branches of government? (executive, legislative, and judicial)

4. Look at page 93. Who was the first President of the United States? (George Washington)

5. Look at page 95. What four things did George Washington accomplish during his terms in office? (He kept the United States out of wars; raised enough money to pay off the country's war debt; established a national bank; and set up a money system.)

Intermediate Level Questions

Encourage students at this level to offer verbal responses or short written responses to the following questions.

1. Look at Section 1. How many representatives were in Congress under the Articles of Confederation? (13)

2. Look at Section 1. When could a territory ask for statehood? (when it reached a population of 60,000)

3. Look at Section 2. What was Roger Sherman's contribution to the Constitution? (the Great Compromise)

4. Look at Section 2. Who were the Federalists and the Anti-Federalists? (The Federalists were wealthy landowners, merchants, and lawyers who supported the Constitution. The Anti-Federalists were mostly farmers who did not support the Constitution.)

5. Look at Section 3. What were George Washington's accomplishments? (He kept the United States out of wars; raised enough money to pay off the country's war debt; established a national bank; and set up a money system.)

Advanced Level Questions

Encourage students at this level to provide written responses in complete sentences to the following questions.

1. Which of the problems listed on page 85 might affect the individual citizens of a state? Explain. (Closing ports would affect people's income; people could not use their money in other states; courts wouldn't be able to settle arguments between individuals in different states.)

2. Why did the delegates from Virginia give more power to larger states? (They felt that states with more people should have more votes in Congress.)

3. Why was the system of checks and balances important? (It made sure that no one branch of government had more power than another.)

4. What were the problems facing George Washington as President? (He had no examples to follow; he had to find money to pay war debts; he had to work out trade agreements with foreign countries; and he had to make decisions that were best for all the states.)

5. What were the Alien and Sedition Acts? (The Alien Act required immigrants to wait 14 years to become citizens. The Sedition Act made it a crime to write or print articles criticizing the government.)

Closing the Chapter

Ask students to use the timeline on pages 82–83 of the Student Edition to summarize what they learned in the chapter.

Chapter 6
Economy and Expansion (1800–1830)
pages 100–117

▶ Introducing the Chapter

Tapping Prior Knowledge

Ask students to preview the chapter by reading the headings and the subheadings and by looking at the art and photos (on pages 100, 103, 105, 110, 112, and 115 of the Student Edition), the timeline (on pages 100–101 of the Student Edition), the map (on page 104 of the Student Edition), the chart (on page 107 of the Student Edition), and the numbered list (on page 108 of the Student Edition). Then, ask students if they can think of one invention that has made a big change in their lives. Encourage students to talk about their personal experiences of change. Ask students, *How did the need for change lead to the Industrial Revolution?*

Preteaching Vocabulary

Personalizing Vocabulary Begin by asking students to preview the chapter for five unfamiliar words or phrases and to record them in their Word Logs. Once students have identified these words and phrases, ask them to use their dictionaries to define them.

Identifying Essential Vocabulary Go over the pronunciation and meaning of each word and phrase in the box below. Then, distribute the Spider Web on page 73 of this guide and ask students to decide which words in the box below are about war, which are about farming, and which are about industry. Ask students to label the spokes of their webs **War, Farming,** and **Industry** and to fill in the webs with the words and phrases from the box below.

Word or Phrase	Meaning
declared war on	announced a fight (p.106)
factory	a place where things are made (p.109)
invented	created or discovered (p.110)
cash crop	fruits and vegetables that make money (p.112)
raising and harvesting	growing and collecting (p.113)

▶ Applying Content Knowledge

From the Chapter: Connecting History and Economics (page 115)

Ask students to read Connecting History and Economics: The Cotton Gin on page 115 of the Student Edition. Then, brainstorm with students other inventions that have made major changes in the economy and in the world. Then, distribute the three-column chart on page 74 of this guide and ask students to write **Invention, Positive Results,** and **Negative Results** for the headings. Have students list the positives and negatives of each invention on their charts. You might wish to ask students to write a paragraph explaining the good and bad side of progress, using this model as a topic sentence: *New inventions have both negative and positive results.*

Positive and Negative Results of Inventions		
Invention	**Positive Results**	**Negative Results**

Using Visuals

Ask students to read pages 110–111 of the Student Edition. Then, have students create a picture dictionary using the names of the mass-produced goods. Ask students to list on a sheet of paper the name of each good and place a picture of that good next to its name. Students may wish draw a picture themselves or cut pictures out of magazines.

Personalizing the Lesson

Review the map on page 104 of the Student Edition and the information about the Lewis and Clark expedition. Ask students to work in groups to list possible fears and the potential excitement these explorers might experience. Ask students, *Would you have liked to go on such an expedition?* Have them write a paragraph giving at least three reasons to explain why they would or would not go on this trip.

Assessing Content Knowledge

Ask students to respond to the following questions. You may wish to encourage students with higher language proficiency to help beginning level students understand the questions.

Beginning Level Questions
Encourage students at this level to think about the answers to these questions and offer short verbal responses.

1. Look at the map on page 104. What rivers did Lewis and Clark travel on? (Missouri and Columbia)

2. Look at page 106. What was the name of the war between the United States and Great Britain? (the War of 1812)

3. Look at page 108. What three points did President Monroe make in his speech? (promised to protect freedom of countries on the American continents; warned Europe not to start new colonies, try to get back old ones, or enlarge any still there; and promised, in return, that the United States would stay out of European problems)

4. Look at page 113. What were four conditions that slaves could face? (working long, hard days in the fields; getting whipped for speaking out or being disobedient; being sold as punishment; being taken away from their families)

5. Look at page 115. What was the cotton gin? (a machine that cleaned 50 pounds of cotton in a day)

Intermediate Level Questions
Encourage students at this level to offer verbal responses or short written responses to the following questions.

1. Look at Section 1. What did Lewis and Clark do for the United States? (explored parts of the Louisiana Purchase)

2. Look at the map on page 104. How did the Louisiana Purchase change the United States? (doubled the size)

3. Look at Section 1. What warning does the Monroe Doctrine give to Europe? (not to start new colonies, try to get back old ones, or enlarge any in the Americas)

4. Look at Section 2. What was the Industrial Revolution? (creation of factories where large numbers of people worked)

5. Look at Section 3. Who was Nat Turner? (a man who led a large slave revolt in Virginia)

Advanced Level Questions
Encourage students at this level to provide written responses in complete sentences to the following questions.

1. What did Lewis and Clark have for President Jefferson after their exploration? (They had maps, as well as plant and animal samples.)

2. What are two reasons why Congress declared war on Great Britain? (Congress declared war on Great Britain because of impressment and because many Americans believed that the British were helping Native Americans attack settlements in the West.)

3. What was the purpose of the Monroe Doctrine? (The purpose of the Monroe Doctrine was to set a policy designed to keep European countries out of the Americas.)

4. What were the different effects that the Industrial Revolution had on the North and on the South? (Answers will vary. Student answers should reflect increased industry in the North and development of the cotton economy in the South.)

5. What were the results of organized revolts by enslaved workers? (They all failed.)

Closing the Chapter

Distribute the Outline on page 75 of this guide. Ask students to outline the chapter using the headings and the subheadings from the chapter. Have students complete the outline by filling in the important details discussed under each heading. Then, ask students to write a paragraph that summarizes what they learned in the chapter.

Chapter 7 / The Changing United States (1820–1850)

pages 118–135

▶ Introducing the Chapter

Tapping Prior Knowledge

Ask students to preview the chapter by reading the headings and subheadings and by looking at the art and photos (on pages 118, 121, 122, 124, 125, 129, 132, and 133 of the Student Edition), the timeline (on pages 118–119 of the Student Edition), the map (on page 127 of the Student Edition), and the numbered list (on page 130 of the Student Edition). Then, direct students to the art on pages 118 and 122. Ask them to think about the trips they have taken and the things that they did to prepare for those trips. Ask students, *What are some of the problems and adventures that the western settlers might have had?*

Preteaching Vocabulary

Personalizing Vocabulary Begin by asking students to preview the chapter for five unfamiliar words or phrases and to record them in their Word Logs. Once students have identified these words and phrases, ask them to use their dictionaries to define them.

Identifying Essential Vocabulary Go over the pronunciation and meaning of each word and phrase in the box below. Then, distribute graph paper with large boxes and ask students to use the words and phrases to create a crossword puzzle. Have students use the sentences from the text as clues.

Word or Phrase	Meaning
common man	everyday person (p.120)
upper class	the highest social group (p.121)
took office	began to serve a political term (p.122)
covered wagon	a cart with a top (p.125)
waterway	path made up of water (p.125)
early 1800s	1800s–1830s (p.126)
strike it rich	get a lot of money (p.133)

▶ Applying Content Knowledge

From the Chapter: History and You (page 132)

Ask students to read History and You: Denim Pants on page 132 of the Student Edition. Ask students, *How many years have people been buying and wearing jeans? What can you conclude about opportunities in America from this family business?* Help students define the term *American Dream*. Encourage students to use their bilingual dictionaries to define the word *American* and then the word *dream*. Ask students, *How is Levi Strauss's story an example of the American Dream?*

Using Visuals

Ask students to review the Geography Fact on page 130 of the Student Edition. Because rivers were so important to settlement, westward expansion, and transportation, provide students with a physical map of North America. Ask students to highlight and label the rivers in the United States. You may wish to refer them to the physical map on page 617 of the Student Edition. Ask students to work in groups to brainstorm benefits that rivers provide for towns and cities.

Personalizing the Lesson

Suggest that students suppose they are traveling across the United States from St. Louis to the Oregon Territory, a 2,000-mile journey that lasted 6 months. Ask students, *What problems and experiences do you think you might have? How is that different from traveling today?* Have each student work with a partner to make a diary of a 2,000-mile trip across the United States in 1840 and another diary of a 2,000-mile trip across the United States today.

Assessing Content Knowledge

Ask students to respond to the following questions. You may wish to encourage students with higher language proficiency to help beginning level students understand the questions.

Beginning Level Questions

Encourage students at this level to think about the answers to these questions and offer short verbal responses.

1. Look at page 120. What did the Tariff of 1828 do? (put a tax on some goods coming in from other countries)

2. Look at pages 125–126. How did people travel in the 1830s? (waterways [rivers and canals], train, wagons)

3. Look at page 130. What war ended with the Treaty of Guadalupe Hidalgo? (the war with Mexico)

4. Look at page 131. What did James Marshall discover at Sutter's Mill? (two gold nuggets)

5. Look at page 133. Who were the forty-niners? (people who went to California to find gold)

Intermediate Level Questions

Encourage students at this level to offer verbal responses or short written responses to the following questions.

1. Look at Section 1. Why did the Tariff of 1828 help Andrew Jackson? (People voted for Jackson instead of Adams.)

2. Look at Section 1. What did Jackson do to the Cherokees? (forced them to give up lands and move west)

3. Look at Section 2. Why were the railroads important? (made travel faster and easier)

4. Look at Section 2. What were the three terms of the Treaty of Guadalupe Hidalgo? (The Mexican government must give up all claims to Texas and to all land between Texas and California; the Rio Grande will become the southern boundary of Texas; and the United States must pay Mexico $15 million for the new land.)

5. Look at Section 3. What was the Gold Rush? (people going to California to find gold in 1849)

Advanced Level Questions

Encourage students at this level to provide written responses in complete sentences to the following questions.

1. What was one of Andrew Jackson's goals once he was elected? (One of Andrew Jackson's goals was to give many ordinary people jobs in government.)

2. What was the purpose of the Indian Removal Act of 1830? (The purpose of the Indian Removal Act of 1830 was to take land away from Native Americans and give it to settlers.)

3. How did the United States acquire the land between Texas and California, including present-day New Mexico and Arizona? (The United States acquired the land as a result of the war with Mexico, which ended with the Treaty of Guadalupe Hidalgo and the Gadsden Purchase.)

4. What was important about the Alamo? (The Alamo was where the Mexicans defeated the Texans.)

5. How did the discovery of gold change California? (The discovery of gold caused the Gold Rush, increased the population, and led to California becoming a state.)

Closing the Chapter

Ask students to summarize the most important points from the chapter by listing all chapter titles and headings and writing a sentence for each. You may wish to ask students to combine their sentences into a one-paragraph summary, using this model as a topic sentence: *Between 1820 and 1850, the United States had many changes.*

Chapter
8

Newcomers and New Ideas (1820–1860)
pages 136–152

▶ Introducing the Chapter

Tapping Prior Knowledge

Ask students to preview the chapter by reading the headings and subheadings and by looking at the art and photos (on pages 136, 139, 144, 146, 147, and 148 of the Student Edition), the timeline (on pages 136–137 of the Student Edition), the chart (on page 143 of the Student Edition), and the numbered list (on page 145 of the Student Edition). Ask students to study the chapter title *Newcomers and New Ideas* on page 137 of the Student Edition. Ask students, *How does a country change when large numbers of people from other countries come to improve their lives?* Encourage students to discuss their experiences or the experiences of people they know who came to the United States. Ask students, *Can our experiences help us understand the experiences of people in the United States in the mid-1800s?*

Preteaching Vocabulary

Personalizing Vocabulary Begin by asking students to preview the chapter for five unfamiliar words or phrases and to record them in their Word Logs. Once students have identified these words and phrases, ask them to use their dictionaries to define them.

Identifying Essential Vocabulary Go over the pronunciation and meaning of each word and phrase in the box below. Then, ask each student to write a sentence for each word and phrase. Ask students to rewrite their sentences, leaving a blank space in place of the vocabulary term. Then, have students exchange sentences with a partner and fill in the blanks in the sentences their partner wrote.

Word or Phrase	Meaning
prevented	stopped or kept from happening (p.139)
in great demand	wanted by many (p.139)
present-day	right now or today (p.140)
make their fortune	make a lot of money (p.141)
swampland	land that is soaked with water (p.141)
made a living	made enough money to survive (p.141)

▶ Applying Content Knowledge

From the Chapter: Voices From the Past (page 146)

Ask students to read Voices From the Past: Elizabeth Cady Stanton on page 146 of the Student Edition. Then, distribute the three-column chart on page 74 of this guide and ask students to label the columns **Advice, Agree/Disagree,** and **Reason.** Have students work in groups to list the advice Elizabeth Cady Stanton gave for raising girls. Ask students to agree or disagree with the advice and to give reasons for their opinions.

Using Resources

Ask students to review the Women Who Worked for Equal Rights chart on page 143 of the Student Edition. Then, ask each student to choose one woman to research on the Internet. Students should find five details about the woman they choose. You may wish to give students markers so that they can record the information they found on a large piece of paper for classroom display.

Organizing Information

Distribute copies of the Idea Web on page 76 of this guide. Use the chapter title, **Newcomers and New Ideas,** as the central topic. Place the headings **New Ways and New People, Women and Political Rights,** and **Working for Reform** in the outer shapes. Then, ask students to list key details that they learned about each heading.

Personalizing the Lesson

Ask students to review Section 3 and write opinions to the following questions: *Should all children be required to attend school? Can education prevent crime and other social problems? Can you be a good citizen if you aren't educated?* Then, ask students to choose one of their opinions and list three reasons to support it.

Assessing Content Knowledge

Ask students to respond to the following questions. You may wish to encourage students with higher language proficiency to help beginning level students understand the questions.

Beginning Level Questions

Encourage students at this level to think about the answers to these questions and offer short verbal responses.

1. Look at page 139. What European countries did many immigrants come from? (Germany and Ireland)

2. Look at page 142. In the early 1800s, what important right did women <u>not</u> have? (suffrage)

3. Look at the chart on page 143. Who were the seven women who worked for equal rights? (Susan B. Anthony; Angelina Grimké; Sarah Grimké; Lucretia Mott; Elizabeth Cady Stanton; Lucy Stone; and Sojourner Truth)

4. Look at page 144. Who was Susan B. Anthony? (a leader in the struggle for women's rights)

5. Look at pages 147–149. What are four reform movements from the early 1800s? (education, use of alcohol, opportunities for women, conditions for mentally ill)

Intermediate Level Questions

Encourage students at this level to offer verbal responses or short written responses to the following questions.

1. Look at Section 1. What are two reasons immigrants came to the United States? (for a better life and for freedom)

2. Look at Section 2. What was the Seneca Falls convention? (the first women's rights convention in the United States)

3. Look at the chart on page 143. What did all seven women have in common? (worked for women's rights)

4. Look at Section 2. What four rights did the 1860 law that was passed in New York give to women? (Married women could own property; women could collect their own wages, sue in court, and enter into contracts.)

5. Look at Section 3. In addition to equal rights, what three things did reformers want to improve in the early 1800s? (education, conditions for the mentally ill, and use of alcohol)

Advanced Level Questions

Encourage students at this level to provide written responses in complete sentences to the following questions.

1. Why did urban areas grow between 1820 and 1850? (People were looking for work and/or the excitement of life in the cities.)

2. How did new inventions change life in the United States? (New inventions reduced the need for farm labor and increased the need for factory workers in the cities, so thousands of farm workers moved to the cities.)

3. What was expected of women in the early 1800s? (Women were expected to be good wives and mothers, and they had few rights that women have today.)

4. How did the Seneca Falls convention affect women's rights? (Women discussed women's rights issues.)

5. What were the four major reform movements in the early 1800s? (The four major reform movements were equal rights, free public education, temperance, and improved conditions for the mentally ill.)

Closing the Chapter

Ask students to use the Idea Web they completed in the Organizing Information activity on page 16 of this guide to write a summary about what they learned in the chapter.

Chapter 9

North and South Disagree (1820–1861)
pages 154–173

▶ Introducing the Chapter

Tapping Prior Knowledge

Ask students to preview the chapter by reading the headings and subheadings and by looking at the art and photos (on pages 153, 154, 163, 167, and 170 of the Student Edition), the timeline (on pages 154–155 of the Student Edition), the numbered lists (on pages 157, 160, and 167 of the Student Edition), the maps (on pages 157 and 161 of the Student Edition), and the chart (on page 159 of the Student Edition). Ask students to suppose that they disagreed with a classmate about how he or she was treating one of your friends. Ask students, *How would you solve the problem?* Encourage students to share examples from their own experiences or study. Ask students, *How does your own experience help you to understand the problems the North and the South were having because they disagreed?*

Preteaching Vocabulary

Personalizing Vocabulary Begin by asking students to preview the chapter for five unfamiliar words or phrases and to record them in their Word Logs. Once students have identified these words and phrases, ask them to use their dictionaries to define them.

Identifying Essential Vocabulary Go over the pronunciation and meaning of each word and phrase in the box below. Then, ask students to write a sentence that gives the word or phrase and its meaning. You may wish to ask students to model the following sentence. *A _____ is an agreement in which everyone takes less than what they wanted at first.* (compromise)

Word or Phrase	Meaning
compromise	agreement; give and take (p.156)
debate	discussion (p.156)
banned	not allowed (p.160)
movement	the act of a group of people to achieve something (p.162)
to turn against	to not agree with someone (p.163)

▶ Applying Content Knowledge

From the Chapter: A Closer Look (page 163)

Ask students to read A Closer Look: The Underground Railroad on page 163 of the Student Edition. Ask students what the risks for these activities were. After a discussion of the dangers and problems involved, ask students to work in pairs to list the qualities Harriet Tubman needed in order to be an Underground Railroad conductor. You might wish to refer students to biographies or Internet articles about Harriet Tubman and other conductors to help them compile their lists.

Using Visuals

Ask students to review Building Your Skills on page 161 of the Student Edition. Ask students, *What are the free states and territories? What are the slave states and territories? What areas were affected by the Missouri Compromise? What areas will be closed to slavery? What areas will be open to slavery? What two areas became states after the Missouri Compromise of 1820? What areas are not owned by the United States?* You might wish to suggest that students work with a partner to compare answers.

Organizing Information

Distribute the Outline on page 75 of this guide. As students read the chapter, ask them to use the outline to fill in the headings and corresponding details.

```
Topic: North and South Disagree
  I. Expansion and Compromise
      A.
      B.
      C.
 II. Northerners Change Their Thinking
      A.
      B.
      C.
III. Troubles Build
      A.
      B.
      C.
```

Assessing Content Knowledge

Ask students to respond to the following questions. You may wish to encourage students with higher language proficiency to help beginning level students understand the questions.

Beginning Level Questions

Encourage students at this level to think about the answers to these questions and offer short verbal responses.

1. Look at page 156. In 1820, how many slave states did the United States have? (twelve)

2. Look at the chart on page 159. What three issues were the 3 regions debating about? (taxes on goods from other countries; immigration to the United States; and slavery in territories and new states)

3. Look at page 162. What did abolitionists want? (to abolish slavery)

4. Look at page 167. Who was Dred Scott? (a slave from Missouri who went to court to ask for his freedom)

5. Look at page 171. What caused the beginning of the U.S. Civil War? (the Confederate's attack on Fort Sumter)

Intermediate Level Questions

Encourage students at this level to offer verbal responses or short written responses to the following questions.

1. Look at Section 1. What were the main points of the Missouri Compromise? (Missouri would enter the Union as a slave state; Maine would enter the Union as a free state; the rest of the Louisiana Territory would be divided by a line, and no slavery would be allowed in the states north of that line.)

2. Look at Section 2. What was the goal of the abolitionists? (to end slavery)

3. Look at Section 2. What was the purpose of the Underground Railroad? (to help African Americans escape to freedom)

4. Look at Section 3. What three things did the Dred Scott decision state? (Scott could not bring a case to court because he was not a U.S. citizen; the law considered slaves property; and the Missouri Compromise was against the law.)

5. Look at Section 3. Why were the Lincoln-Douglas debates important? (They led to Lincoln becoming President.)

Advanced Level Questions

Encourage students at this level to provide written responses in complete sentences to the following questions.

1. What was the purpose of the Missouri Compromise? (It kept the balance between slave and free states in the Senate as territories in the Louisiana Purchase became states.)

2. What were two actions that abolitionists took against slavery? (Abolitionists started an anti-slavery newspaper, and they worked together to set up the Underground Railroad.)

3. What are two reasons the Dred Scott Case was important? (The Supreme Court declared the Missouri Compromise unconstitutional, and it opened all territories to slavery.)

4. Why did Southerners feel powerless after the election of 1860? (Lincoln was elected even though he did not win any southern states.)

5. Beginning with the election of 1860, what are four steps that led to the Civil War? (Four steps that led to the Civil War include Lincoln's election, states seceded, southern states took over forts, and Fort Sumter fell.)

Closing the Chapter

Ask students to use the outline they completed for the Organizing Information activity on page 18 of this guide to summarize what they learned in the chapter.

Chapter 10 · The Civil War (1861–1865)

▶ Introducing the Chapter

Tapping Prior Knowledge

Ask students to preview the chapter by reading the headings and subheadings and by looking at the art and photos (on pages 174, 182, 184, 187, and 189 of the Student Edition), the timeline (on pages 174–175 of the Student Edition), the charts (on pages 177 and 191 of the Student Edition), the numbered lists (on pages 178 and 192 of the Student Edition), and the map (on page 180 of the Student Edition). Ask students if the countries from which they or their families came experienced war or conflict. Ask students, *How can our present-day knowledge help us understand wars from the past?*

Preteaching Vocabulary

Personalizing Vocabulary Begin by asking students to preview the chapter for five unfamiliar words or phrases and to record them in their Word Logs. Once students have identified these words and phrases, ask them to use their dictionaries to define them.

Identifying Essential Vocabulary Go over the pronunciation and meaning of each word and phrase in the box below. Then, have students create a chart using the following headings: **Word or Phrase, Clues from the Text, Definition, How Can I Remember the Meaning**, and **My Sentence**. Students may choose to draw a picture or use a brief explanation in the **How Can I Remember the Meaning** column.

Word or Phrase	Meaning
blockade	something that stops movement (p.178)
cannonball	an object that is shot from a cannon (p.181)
supply route	a path used for the delivery of goods (p.182)
drafting	selecting a group for a special reason (p.185)
march	walk or journey (p.191)
terms of surrender	rules for giving up (p.192)

▶ Applying Content Knowledge

From the Chapter: Connecting History and Technology (page 189)

Ask students to read Connecting History and Technology: The Technology of War on page 189 of the Student Edition. Then, ask students to list the inventions that were used for the first time in war. Ask students, *What does the phrase* inventions move the world *mean?* Encourage students to use their bilingual dictionaries to define any words in the expression that may be unfamiliar. Have students suggest possible meanings of the phrase and work with students to arrive at a clear explanation of the phrase. Then, ask students, *How do inventions move the world?*

Organizing Information

Distribute copies of the Idea Web on page 76 of this guide. As students read the chapter, ask them to fill in the Idea Web. Use the chapter title, **The Civil War,** as the central topic. Place the headings **Preparing for War, The Early Years of War, Life at Home,** and **The End of the War** in the outer shapes. Then, ask students to list key details that they learned about each heading.

Using Visuals

Distribute index cards to each student. Ask students to look at the Major Battles of the Civil War chart on page 191 of the Student Edition. Have students work with a partner to create questions about the battles. Ask students to write one question on the front of an index card and the answer to that question on the back of the index card. Then, have all students place their cards in one box or bowl. Divide the class into two groups. Choose cards from the box or bowl, read them aloud, and have students answer the questions.

▶ Assessing Content Knowledge

Ask students to respond to the following questions. You may wish to encourage students with higher language proficiency to help beginning level students understand the questions.

Beginning Level Questions

Encourage students at this level to think about the answers to these questions and offer short verbal responses.

1. Look at page 177. Where was the first big battle of the war? (Battle of Bull Run)

2. Look at the map on page 180. How many battles did each side win? (Confederate: 4; Union: 11)

3. Look at page 183. Which battle was the turning point of the Civil War? (the Battle of Gettysburg)

4. Look at page 186. What was the Emancipation Proclamation? (a public statement that freed enslaved African Americans in the rebelling states)

5. Look at the chart on page 191. What information does the third column of the chart tell? (where each battle took place)

Intermediate Level Questions

Encourage students at this level to offer verbal responses or short written responses to the following questions.

1. Look at Section 1. What were the strengths of the North and the South? (See the chart on page 177.)

2. Look at Section 1. What were the three main goals of the Anaconda Plan? (blockade the southern ports; attack the South along the Mississippi River to split the Confederacy in two; and continue to attack the Confederates in the East)

3. Look at Section 2. Why was the Battle of Gettysburg the turning point of the war? (The Confederate Army was badly beaten and would never be strong enough to attack the North again.)

4. Look at Section 3. What did Lincoln do to ban slavery in the rebelling states? (issued the Emancipation Proclamation)

5. Look at Section 4. When Grant and Lee met in 1865, what terms did they agree to? (Southern soldiers must give up their weapons but could keep the horses or mules they owned. Southern officers could keep their weapons and horses. All southern soldiers would be fed.)

Advanced Level Questions

Encourage students at this level to provide written responses in complete sentences to the following questions.

1. Look at the chart on page 177. Which was stronger, the North or the South? (The North was stronger than the South because it had more men, money, factories, and railroads.)

2. Why did President Lincoln and other Union leaders develop the Anaconda Plan? (They developed the Anaconda Plan to squeeze the Confederacy.)

3. What was General Grant's strategy for winning the war? (He would attack Lee. Sherman would march from Atlanta to the Atlantic Ocean. The North would use total war against the South.)

4. By 1865, why was the Confederacy unable to fight anymore? (The Confederacy was unable to fight because it was running out of troops and supplies.)

5. What was the cost of the war in people and money? (The cost of the war in people was 618,000 men killed, and 375,000 men wounded. The Union spent $8 billion, and the Confederacy spent $2 billion.)

▶ Closing the Chapter

Ask students to use the Idea Web they completed for the Organizing Information activity on page 20 of this guide to write a summary about what they learned in the chapter.

Chapter 11

Rebuilding a Divided Nation (1865–1877)
pages 196–213

▶ Introducing the Chapter

Tapping Prior Knowledge

Ask students to preview the chapter by reading the headings and the subheadings and by looking at the art and photos (on pages 196, 199, 200, 203, 204, 207, and 211 of the Student Edition), the timeline (on pages 196–197 of the Student Edition), and the numbered lists (on pages 198 and 201 of the Student Edition). Ask students to suppose that they wanted to repair a relationship with a friend or relative that had been damaged. Ask them to suggest some of the issues that would need to be addressed and how they might rebuild the relationship. Ask students, *Why can rebuilding an entire nation be difficult?*

Preteaching Vocabulary

Personalizing Vocabulary Begin by asking students to preview the chapter for five unfamiliar words or phrases and to record them in their Word Logs. Once students have identified these words and phrases, ask them to use their dictionaries to define them.

Identifying Essential Vocabulary Go over the pronunciation and meaning of each word and phrase in the box below. Then, ask students to look at the word *destroyed*. Explain that the word comes in many forms: *destroy, destruction,* and *destructive*. For example, *destroyed* is the past tense of the verb *destroy; destruction* is a noun; and *destructive* is an adjective. Tell students that the words *ruin, loyalty, effect,* and *prevent* also have many different forms.

Word or Phrase	Meaning
destroyed	wrecked or ruined (p.196)
in ruins	broken (p.198)
loyalty oath	a promise made to show duty (p.198)
into effect	in the process of happening (p.199)
hanged	a way to be killed (p.200)
prevent	keep from happening (p.201)
bureau	a group that gives special information about something (p.206)

▶ Applying Content Knowledge

From the Chapter: Voices From the Past (page 211)

Ask students to read Voices From the Past: Tempie Cummins on page 211 of the Student Edition. You might wish to read the third paragraph aloud to the students. Then, have students work in groups to decide (infer) the emotions Tempie's mother felt after she learned she was free. Suggest that they read Tempie's story carefully to find evidence that supports their inferences.

Organizing Information

Distribute the four-column chart on page 70 of this guide. Ask students to label the columns **Lincoln, Johnson, Radical Republicans,** and **Similarities/Differences.** To help students understand the different plans for Reconstruction, ask students to complete the chart by listing the plans of Lincoln, Johnson, and the Radical Republicans. Then, have students record the similarities and differences between the three plans in the fourth column.

Using Visuals

Ask students to review pages 206–207 of the Student Edition and study the art on page 207 of the Student Edition. Distribute the Venn diagram on page 77 of this guide. Ask students to label the sections **Today's Schools, Both,** and **Freedmen's Bureau Schools.** Then, have students compare and contrast today's schools and Freedmen Bureau Schools by listing details in the appropriate sections of the diagram. Ask students to use their completed Venn diagrams to write a summary. Students may wish to use this model as a topic sentence: *Schools today are very different from the schools taught by the Freedmen's Bureau after the Civil War.*

Assessing Content Knowledge

Ask students to respond to the following questions. You may wish to encourage students with higher language proficiency to help beginning level students understand the questions.

Beginning Level Questions

Encourage students at this level to think about the answers to these questions and offer short verbal responses.

1. Look at page 200. What were the black codes? (laws that took away many rights of freed African Americans)

2. Look at page 202. Who passed the Reconstruction Acts? (Radical Republicans in Congress)

3. Look at page 203. What does it mean to impeach a President? (to accuse him of a crime)

4. Look at page 209. What did the Fifteenth Amendment say? (The right of a person to vote could not be denied "on account of race, color, or previous conditions of servitude.")

5. Look at page 210. What did the segregation laws do? (separated whites and African Americans)

Intermediate Level Questions

Encourage students at this level to offer verbal responses or short written responses to the following questions.

1. Look at Section 1. What was the purpose of the black codes? (to restrict the rights of freed African Americans)

2. Look at Section 2. What did the Reconstruction Act of 1867 say? (All states that did not accept the Fourteenth Amendment would be under military rule; all adult African American males and all qualified adult white males could vote; and whites who held Confederate office or supported the Confederacy could not vote.)

3. Look at Section 2. Why did the Radical Republicans impeach President Johnson? (because his actions made them angry)

4. Look at Section 3. What was the reason for the Fifteenth Amendment? (to ensure that African Americans could vote)

5. Look at Section 3. What was the purpose of the Jim Crow laws? (The Jim Crow laws kept African Americans and whites separate.)

Advanced Level Questions

Encourage students at this level to provide written responses in complete sentences to the following questions.

1. What did the Civil Rights Act of 1866 say? (The Civil Rights Act of 1866 said that African Americans should have the same legal rights as white Americans.)

2. Why did Congress pass the Reconstruction Acts? (Congress passed the Reconstruction Acts to force the Southern states to give rights to African Americans.)

3. What important role did the Freedmen's Bureau play? (The Freedmen's Bureau played an important role in starting schools for African Americans who has been enslaved.)

4. What were some of the changes in the lives of African Americans after the war? (After the war, African Americans left the plantations to look for family members who had been sold; couples were married legally; children went to school; and some African Americans found jobs.)

5. What action ended Reconstruction? (The withdrawal of troops from the South ended Reconstruction.)

Closing the Chapter

Ask students to use the timeline on pages 196–197 of the Student Edition to write a summary about what they learned in the chapter.

Chapter 12

Americans Move West (1860–1890)
pages 216–233

Introducing the Chapter

Tapping Prior Knowledge

Ask students to preview the chapter by reading the headings and subheadings and by looking at the art and photos (on pages 215, 216, 219, 220, 223, 224, 225, and 228 of the Student Edition), the timeline (on pages 216–217 of the Student Edition), the numbered list (on pages 224–225 of the Student Edition), the chart (on page 228 of the Student Edition), and the map (on page 229 of the Student Edition). Ask students if they, or anyone they know, have ever moved from one place to another. Encourage students to share their experiences or the experiences of people they know. Ask students, *How might our discussion help us understand what the Americans' move west was like?*

Preteaching Vocabulary

Personalizing Vocabulary Begin by asking students to preview the chapter for five unfamiliar words or phrases and to record them in their Word Logs. Once students have identified these words and phrases, ask them to use their dictionaries to define them.

Identifying Essential Vocabulary Go over the pronunciation and meaning of each word and phrase in the box below. Then, distribute the four-column chart on page 70 of this guide. Ask students to label the columns **Word or Phrase, Sentence From the Text, Synonym,** and **My Sentence.** Ask students to complete their charts using their bilingual dictionaries and the words and phrases from the box below.

Word or Phrase	Meaning
entire	the whole thing (p.218)
drove	pushed (p.219)
soil	dirt; earth (p.220)
broken promise	something that someone said they would do that they don't do (p.222)
set aside	gave; assigned (p.222)
rounded up	collected (p.228)

Applying Content Knowledge

From the Chapter: Building Your Skills (page 221)

Ask students to read Building Your Skills: Distinguishing Fact From Opinion on page 221 of the Student Edition. Provide magazines and newspapers with ads for students and ask them to choose a favorite ad. Have students identify sentences in the ad that they think are facts and circle them. Then, have students identify sentences that they think are opinions and underline them. Have students discuss how they made their decisions.

Organizing Information

Ask students to review Section 3. Distribute the Main Idea and Supporting Details chart on page 78 of this guide. Have students write **Life on the Great Plains** in the Main Idea box and **Cattle Business, Mining,** and **Farming** in each of the Supporting Details boxes. Ask students to add two or three word details on the life of the cowhand, the miner, and the farmer.

Using Visuals

After students finish reading the chapter, ask them to review the map on page 229 of the Student Edition. Ask students, *What four trails are shown on the map? What were these trails used for?* Students should understand that the Goodnight-Loving Trail, the Western Trail, the Chisholm Trail, and the Sedalia Trail were all cattle trails. You may wish to ask students other questions about the map, such as: *What states did the Sedalia Trail go through?* and *How many states did the Goodnight-Loving Trail go through?*

Assessing Content Knowledge

Ask students to respond to the following questions. You may wish to encourage students with higher language proficiency to help beginning level students understand the questions.

Beginning Level Questions

Encourage students at this level to think about the answers to these questions and offer short verbal responses.

1. Look at the picture on page 219. What is happening in the picture? (The men are completing the transcontinental railroad.)

2. Look at page 220. What was a homesteader? (a person who received land under the Homestead Act of 1862)

3. Look at pages 223–224. What are the names of two Native American groups? (Possible answers include Cheyenne, Arapaho, Lakota, and Nez Percé.)

4. Look at the chart on page 228. What are three things about a cowhand's life on a cattle drive? (Possible answers include their hours of work, food, special clothing, sleeping quarters, and wages.)

5. Look at page 230. What were the prospectors searching for? (gold, silver, and other valuable minerals)

Intermediate Level Questions

Encourage students at this level to offer verbal responses or short written responses to the following questions.

1. Look at Section 1. Why was the transcontinental railroad important? (It made it easier to travel to the West.)

2. Look at Section 1. What did the Homestead Act of 1862 do? (It gave men who were at least 21 years old 160 acres of land for $10. They had to settle on the land for five years, build a home within six months, and grow crops.)

3. Look at Section 2. Why were the buffalo important for Native Americans but a problem for railroads? (Native Americans used it for food, clothing, and blankets, but the large buffalo ruined the railroad tracks and kept the trains from moving along the rails.)

4. Look at Section 2. What were two incidents when U.S. soldiers killed Native American men, women, and children? (Wounded Knee and Sand Creek)

5. Look at Section 3. What was the Grange? (an organization of farmers formed in 1867 to help one another)

Advanced Level Questions

Encourage students at this level to provide written responses in complete sentences to the following questions.

1. What was the purpose of the Homestead Act of 1862? (The purpose of the Homestead Act was to encourage farmers to move west.)

2. Why do you think the U.S. government wanted people to move west? (Answers will vary. Students' answers might include ideas about occupying the land that the United States had acquired, putting families who would not want slavery into the western territories, or expanding the country.)

3. Why did Native Americans fight to protect their land? (They did not want to leave their homes or lose their traditions.)

4. Look at the map on page 229. Which states and territories had mines? (See the map on page 229 of the Student Edition.)

5. What was the purpose of the Grange? (The purpose of the Grange was to help farmers.)

Closing the Chapter

Ask students to summarize the most important points from the chapter by working in pairs to write each Learning Objective on page 217 as a question and answer. You may wish to suggest that students use large index cards, putting each question on one side of a card and the corresponding answer on the other side.

Chapter 13

The Growth of Industry (1860–1900)

pages 234–251

▶ Introducing the Chapter

Tapping Prior Knowledge

Ask students to preview the chapter by reading the headings and subheadings and by looking at the art and photos (on pages 234, 236, 238, 240, 241, 242, 244, 247, and 248 of the Student Edition), the timeline (on pages 234–235 of the Student Edition), the chart (on page 237 of the Student Edition), and the numbered list (on page 243 of the Student Edition). Ask students what the phrase *growth of industry* means. Encourage students to use their bilingual dictionaries to define any words in the expression that may be unfamiliar. Have students suggest possible meanings of the phrase and work with students to arrive at a clear definition. Then, ask students, *What are examples of industry in the country that you or your family comes from? How does industry growth affect a country?*

Preteaching Vocabulary

Personalizing Vocabulary Begin by asking students to preview the chapter for five unfamiliar words or phrases and to record them in their Word Logs. Once students have identified these words and phrases, ask them to use their dictionaries to define them.

Identifying Essential Vocabulary Go over the pronunciation and meaning of each word and phrase in the box below. Then, ask students to classify each of the following phrases as a noun (n.), noun phrase (n.p.), a verb (v.), or a verb phrase (v.p.).

Word or Phrase	Meaning
grant (n.)	money that is given that does not need to be paid back (p.236)
drilled (v.)	dug with a special tool (p.238)
rusted (v.)	worn away (p.239)
turning out (v.p.)	making; producing (p.239)
left alone (v.p.)	did not bother (p.242)
interfere (v.)	to get involved (p.243)
work force (n.p.)	a group of people who do a job (p.245)
12-hour shifts (n.p.)	work days that last 12 hours (p.245)

▶ Applying Content Knowledge

From the Chapter: Some American Inventions, 1865–1893 (page 237)

Ask students to review the Some American Inventions chart on page 237 of the Student Edition that lists important inventions of the late 1800s. Ask students to think about how many of those inventions we still depend on today. Suggest that students create an additional column for the chart on a separate sheet of paper that shows the things we use today that have replaced or improved upon the original invention. Ask students, *How do each of these items affect our lives?*

Organizing Information

Distribute copies of the Outline on page 75 of this guide. As students read the chapter, ask them to use the outline to fill in the headings and corresponding details.

Personalizing the Lesson

Ask students to work with a partner to read each question below. Then, have them suppose that they are living in the mid- to late 1800s. Distribute the four-column chart on page 70 of this guide and ask students to label the columns **Question, Opinion, 1st Reason of Support,** and **2nd Reason of Support.** Ask students to write the following questions under the heading **Question.** Then, have students write an opinion for each question and give two reasons to support their opinions.

Question 1: Should government leave businesses alone or control some actions of business? (page 242)

Question 2: Should children under 13 work? (page 247)

Question 3: Should women receive the same pay as men if they are doing the same work? (page 246)

Question 4: Should workers go on strike if they think the company is unfair? (page 249)

▶ Assessing Content Knowledge

Ask students to respond to the following questions. You may wish to encourage students with higher language proficiency to help beginning level students understand the questions.

Beginning Level Questions

Encourage students at this level to think about the answers to these questions and offer short verbal responses.

1. Look at page 236. Who was Thomas Edison? (an inventor)

2. Look at the chart on page 237. What information does the third column tell? (the names of inventors)

3. Look at pages 241–242. What did Rockefeller and Carnegie control? (Rockefeller controlled oil, and Carnegie controlled steel.)

4. Look at page 240. What were robber barons? (rich business owners who paid low wages)

5. Look at the picture on page 247. Why do you think boys under 13 worked? (Answers will vary. Students' answers should include issues of need, poverty, and absence of laws.)

Intermediate Level Questions

Encourage students at this level to offer verbal responses or short written responses to the following questions.

1. Look at Section 1. What are three benefits of the electric light bulb? (They made people on city streets feel safe; large buildings could be lighted with less danger of fire; and rooms and halls were made brighter at night.)

2. Look at Section 1. Why was oil drilling like the gold rush? (People drilled for oil just as they had mined for gold, hoping to strike it rich.)

3. Look at Section 2. What are three laws that Congress passed to control big business? (Railroads that traveled through several states had to set prices that were fair to everyone; railroads had to make the prices they charged public; and large companies could not interfere with smaller companies.)

4. Look at Section 2. Why were rich business owners called robber barons? (They got rich [barons] at the expense of poor workers.)

5. Look at Section 3. What were the unsafe working conditions in most factories? (poor lighting, little fresh air, dangerous machinery, and 12-hour shifts)

Advanced Level Questions

Encourage students at this level to provide written responses in complete sentences to the following questions.

1. Why was oil important? (Oil was important because it helped machines run smoothly and was used for lighting lamps and heating homes.)

2. Why was steel important? (Steel was important because it was used in most tall buildings, bridges, and railroad tracks.)

3. Why is a business monopoly unfair? (A business monopoly is unfair because it can control prices.)

4. Why was growing business good for people who wanted to work? (Growing business meant a growing need for workers.)

5. How did labor unions help workers? (Labor unions worked to get higher pay and better working conditions for workers.)

▶ Closing the Chapter

Ask students to use the outline they created for the Organizing Information activity on page 26 of this guide to write a summary of what they learned in the chapter.

ESL/ELL

Chapter 14

Cities and Immigration (1880–1920)
pages 252–269

▶ Introducing the Chapter

Tapping Prior Knowledge

Ask students to preview the chapter by reading the headings and subheadings and by looking at the art and photos (on pages 252, 256, 258, and 260 of the Student Edition), the timeline (on pages 252–253 of the Student Edition), the numbered lists (on pages 255 and 266 of the Student Edition), the chart (on page 255 of the Student Edition), and the map (on page 266 of the Student Edition). Then, direct students to the picture on page 252 in the Student Edition. Have them suppose that they are immigrants coming to America in 1900, who can bring one trunk. Ask students to make a list of the things they would bring in their trunk. Ask students, *How does this discussion help you to understand the experience of immigrants in the late 1800s?*

Preteaching Vocabulary

Personalizing Vocabulary Begin by asking students to preview the chapter for five unfamiliar words or phrases and to record them in their Word Logs. Once students have identified these words and phrases, ask them to use their dictionaries to define them.

Identifying Essential Vocabulary Go over the pronunciation and meaning of each word and phrase in the box below. Then, ask students to work with a partner to write the sentence where they find the word or phrase in the chapter and then replace the word or phrase with a word with which they are familiar. Students may wish to consult their bilingual dictionaries as they rewrite the sentences.

Word or Phrase	Meaning
gateway	a place to enter through (p.256)
skilled workers	people who know how to do a job (p.256)
target	mark; point (p.257)
poorly lit	without enough light (p.258)
ban	to not allow (p.263)
lynched	killed; murdered (p.265)

▶ Applying Content Knowledge

From the Chapter: History Fact (page 257)

Ask students to read the History Fact margin note on page 257 of the Student Edition. Then, distribute the three-column chart on page 74 of this guide. Ask students to create a chart entitled **Birthplaces** with the headings **Students**, **Parents**, and **Grandparents**. Tell students to complete their charts by interviewing the other students in the class to determine birthplace for each family's generation. After they complete their interviews, you may wish to ask students to write concluding sentences based on totals of birthplaces. Students can model their concluding sentences after this example: *One in four students' grandparents were born in another country.*

Organizing Information

Distribute the **KWL** chart on page 79 of this guide. Before you begin to study each section, allow students to complete the **K** and the **W** columns of the chart for that section. Ask students, *What would you like to learn in this section?* Have students complete the **L** column of the chart once they have completed the section of the chapter.

Using Visuals

Ask students to study the Where Immigrants Came From chart on page 255 of the Student Edition. Tell students to write the information from each pie chart as sentences. For example, *Between 1861 and 1880, 7 percent of immigrants came from Southern and Eastern Europe.* You may also wish to ask students to translate the information from the pie charts into bar graphs.

Note-taking

Distribute the Spider Web on page 73 of this guide. Ask students to review the chapter and take notes about the various groups and the rights they fought for. Have students place each group in a separate section of the Spider Web along with their notes about that group.

Assessing Content Knowledge

Ask students to respond to the following questions. You may wish to encourage students with higher language proficiency to help beginning level students understand the questions.

Beginning Level Questions

Encourage students at this level to think about the answers to these questions and offer short verbal responses.

1. Look at page 255. What are three reasons immigrants came to the United States? (wars, violence, and religious freedom)

2. Look at the chart on page 255. What do the numbers in the green areas tell? (how many immigrants came from Southern and Eastern Europe)

3. Look at pages 261–262. What countries did Asian immigrants come from? (China, Japan, Philippines)

4. Look carefully at the map on page 266. How many states lost African Americans, and how many states gained African Americans? (15 lost; 7 gained)

5. Look at page 267. What were three schools for African Americans that opened in the late 1800s? (Howard University, Hampton Institute, Tuskegee Institute)

Intermediate Level Questions

Encourage students at this level to offer verbal responses or short written responses to the following questions.

1. Look at Section 1. What were tenements like? (poorly built, cramped; dirty; noisy; and had little light or air)

2. Look at Section 1. Why did the Triangle Shirtwaist Company fire kill so many people? (The doors were locked, and ladders were too short to reach the eighth floor.)

3. Look at Section 2. What caused feelings of nativism for many Americans? (Many Americans believed that the immigrants were taking jobs from them.)

4. Look at Section 2. What were two steps taken by the U.S. government to limit immigration? (It passed the Chinese Exclusion Act of 1882, and it made a "Gentleman's Agreement" with Japan.)

5. Look at Section 3. What is the NAACP? (the National Association for the Advancement of Colored People, which is a group that fights for equal rights)

Advanced Level Questions

Encourage students at this level to provide written responses in complete sentences to the following questions.

1. What problems did immigrants entering the United States have? (Most immigrants did not speak English; most were not skilled workers; and many did not have enough money to buy land to farm.)

2. Why did the areas where immigrants settled become known as ghettos? (The areas where many immigrants settled became known as ghettos because they were neighborhoods where people of the same race, religion, or country lived.)

3. How did new technology, such as steel, electricity, and building materials, change the cities? (Answers will vary. Students' answers should reflect an awareness that cities could grow through technological advancements.)

4. What kind of jobs did new immigrants have? (Answers will vary. See pages 261 and 264 of the Student Edition.)

5. How were the problems of African Americans different in the North and in the South? (Answers will vary. Students' answers should reflect the fact that discrimination/racism was more severe in the South. For example, in the South, they might be beaten or lynched, and they could not vote.)

Closing the Chapter

Ask students to use the KWL charts that they created for the Organizing Information activity on page 28 of this guide to write a summary about what they learned.

Chapter 15 / The Reformers (1870–1920)

pages 272–289

▶ Introducing the Chapter

Tapping Prior Knowledge

Ask students to preview the chapter by reading the headings and the subheadings and by looking at the art and photos (on pages 271, 272, 276, 280, 281, and 283 of the Student Edition), the timeline (on pages 272–273), the numbered list (on page 285 of the Student Edition), and the map (on page 286 of the Student Edition). Then, ask students to think of situations that need change. Ask students, *Will there always be a need for reform? Why would people want to change things in government and business?*

Preteaching Vocabulary

Personalizing Vocabulary Begin by asking students to preview the chapter for five unfamiliar words or phrases and to record them in their Word Logs. Once students have identified these words and phrases, ask them to use their dictionaries to define them.

Identifying Essential Vocabulary Go over the pronunciation and meaning of each word and phrase in the box below. Then, ask students to look at the word *favor*. Explain that the word comes in many forms like *favored*, *favorable*, *favorite*, and *favoritism*. For example, *favored*, *favorable*, and *favorite* are adjectives; *favorite* and *favoritism* are nouns. Tell students that *corrupt*, *basis*, *movement*, and *authorized* also have many different forms.

Word or Phrase	Meaning
corrupt	not honest (p.275)
favor	something done for someone (p.275)
basis	the part that everything is built on (p.277)
movement	a group of people with a special goal (p.279)
run-down	in bad condition (p.282)
party	a political group of people with common goals (p.284)
authorized	allowed (p.284)
picket line	a line of people who are complaining about something (p.286)

▶ Applying Content Knowledge

From the Chapter: A Closer Look (page 276)

Ask students to read A Closer Look: Political Cartoons on page 276 of the Student Edition. Explain to students that there are different categories of cartoons, which include business cartoons, political cartoons, social cartoons, or economic cartoons. Ask students to define what each of these is using their bilingual dictionaries. Work with students to arrive at a set of criteria that defines each category. Then, ask students to work in small groups to collect newspaper, Internet, and magazine cartoons and group and classify them as business cartoons, political cartoons, social cartoons, or economic cartoons. Ask students, *What makes a cartoon business-related? Political? Social? Economic?*

Organizing Information

Ask students to read Identifying Cause and Effect on page 278 of the Student Edition. Brainstorm with students words used to indicate cause-effect relationships (cause: *because, so, therefore, if, since;* effect: *result, outcome, then, as a result*). Ask students to read the paragraphs on women's suffrage on pages 285–286 of the Student Edition. Have students find two sentences that use cause-effect words, and then have them rewrite three sentences using cause-effect words. You may wish to distribute the Cause and Effect chart on page 80 of this guide for students to take notes on as they read the paragraphs.

Using Visuals

Ask students to study the map on women's suffrage on page 286 of the Student Edition. Review the key and locate the state that students live in. Then, have them identify the states and the dates when each granted full suffrage to women. You may wish to distribute the Timeline on page 72 of this guide and have students record the dates on the timeline. Ask students to suggest reasons that full suffrage was given in western states, but not in most eastern and southern states.

Assessing Content Knowledge

Ask students to respond to the following questions. You may wish to encourage students with higher language proficiency to help beginning level students understand the questions.

Beginning Level Questions

Encourage students at this level to think about the answers to these questions and offer short verbal responses.

1. Look at the timeline on page 272. What two events occurred in 1901? (William McKinley was assassinated, and Theodore Roosevelt took office.)

2. Look at page 275. Who was Boss Tweed? (a political boss in New York City who was corrupt)

3. Look at pages 280–281. Who were three muckrakers? (Upton Sinclair, Ida Tarbell, and Lincoln Steffens)

4. Look at page 284. What was the Sixteenth Amendment to the Constitution? (It authorized the federal income tax.)

5. Look at page 287. What was Prohibition? (a time when it was illegal to sell or transport alcohol in the United States)

Intermediate Level Questions

Encourage students at this level to offer verbal responses or short written responses to the following questions.

1. Look at Section 1. Who were two business leaders that people thought were corrupt? (John D. Rockefeller and Cornelius Vanderbilt)

2. Look at Section 1. What were the corrupt actions of Boss Tweed? (bribes, kickbacks, and theft)

3. Look at Section 2. What did the muckrakers do? (wrote to bring attention to corruption)

4. Look at Section 2. What is trust busting? (breaking large companies into smaller companies so they couldn't force smaller companies out of business)

5. Look at Section 3. Why did some people want alcohol to be illegal? (They felt it was a dangerous and deadly drug that destroyed people and families.)

Advanced Level Questions

Encourage students at this level to provide written responses in complete sentences to the following questions.

1. What were two reforms that Congress passed after Roosevelt was elected? (Possible answers: Reforms cleared run-down areas of cities, made factories safer, controlled power of railroads, and mandated inspection of meatpacking plants.)

2. How did Boss Tweed control elections? (Boss Tweed controlled elections through bribes, favors, and gifts in return for votes.)

3. How did the Civil Service Act reform civil service? (The Civil Service Act required people to pass a test for government jobs.)

4. Why were muckrakers important? (They called attention to corruption.)

5. Why did gangs and crime increase during Prohibition? (There was a lot of money to be made in the unlawful alcohol business.)

Closing the Chapter

Distribute the four-column chart on page 70 of this guide. Have students label the columns **Name of President, Reforms Made Under This President, Constitutional Amendment Passed During His Administration,** and **Issues Changed by the Constitutional Amendment.** Ask students to write the names of the presidents discussed in this chapter under the heading **Name of President.** Ask students to complete the chart for each of the presidents for this period. Explain to students that they may not be able to complete all columns for all Presidents. For example, President Rutherford Hayes proposed a plan for reform, but no constitutional amendment was passed during his administration. Ask students to use their completed charts to write a summary about what they learned.

Chapter 16

Expansion Overseas (1890–1914)

pages 290–307

▶ Introducing the Chapter

Tapping Prior Knowledge

Ask students to preview the chapter by reading the headings and subheadings and by looking at the art and photos (on pages 290, 294, 295, 298, 299, and 301 of the Student Edition), the timeline (on pages 290–291), and the map (on page 304 of the Student Edition). Ask students what the phrase *expansion overseas* means. Encourage students to use their bilingual dictionaries to define any words in the expression that may be unfamiliar. Have students suggest possible meanings of the phrase and work with students to arrive at a clear definition. Then, ask students, *Why might overseas expansion be important?*

Preteaching Vocabulary

Personalizing Vocabulary Begin by asking students to preview the chapter for five unfamiliar words or phrases and to record them in their Word Logs. Once students have identified these words and phrases, ask them to use their dictionaries to define them.

Identifying Essential Vocabulary Go over the pronunciation and meaning of each word and phrase in the box below. Then, ask each student to write a sentence for each word. Ask students to rewrite their sentences, leaving a blank space in place of the vocabulary term. Have students trade sentences with a partner and fill in the blanks in the sentences their partner wrote.

Word or Phrase	Meaning
political affairs	official business (p.292)
expand	spread; make bigger (p.292)
folly	something silly (p.294)
tour	trip; journey (p.296)
exaggerated	make something bigger than it is (p.297)
stationed	positioned; located (p.299)
right-of-way	a path someone is allowed to take (p.303)
treaty	agreement (p.304)

▶ Applying Content Knowledge

From the Chapter: Voices From the Past (page 301)

Ask students to read Voices From the Past: José Martí on page 301 of the Student Edition. Tell students that Martí was a hero in Cuba. Ask students to share information about heroes in their countries. *Why are they heroes? What makes a hero different from others?* Then, distribute the Venn diagram on page 77 of this guide. Ask students to label the sections **José Martí, Both**, and **My Hero** (the name of a hero from their country). Then, have students compare and contrast José Martí with the hero they chose. Have students use their completed Venn diagrams to write a summary. Students may wish to begin their paragraphs with the following sentence: *José Martí and _____ are similar to each other because …*

Organizing Information

Provide a large piece of butcher paper. Ask students to combine timelines for Chapters 12, 13, 14, 15, and 16 to create a new timeline that lists all events from 1890 to 1914. Suggest that students include events in Chapter 16 that are not listed on the timeline, such as the Hawaiian revolt, the Spanish American War, the Treaty of Paris, and the Roosevelt Corollary.

Personalizing the Lesson

Ask students to think about a worker's life during the building of the Panama Canal. Have them write a paragraph describing the work, the conditions, the visit by President Roosevelt, and what will happen when the canal is finished. You may wish to invite volunteers to read their essays to the class after they are complete.

Assessing Content Knowledge

Ask students to respond to the following questions. You may wish to encourage students with higher language proficiency to help beginning level students understand the questions.

Beginning Level Questions

Encourage students at this level to think about the answers to these questions and offer short verbal responses.

1. Look at page 294. Who was the queen of Hawaii from 1891–1893? (Queen Liliuokalani)

2. Look at page 295. What country did the United States ask to have an Open Door Policy for trade? (China)

3. Look at page 298. What happened to the U.S. battleship *Maine*? (It exploded, killing 260 American sailors.)

4. Look at page 299. What did the Treaty of Paris do to the war? (ended it)

5. Look at the map on page 304. Why was the Panama Canal important? (It created a passageway between North America and South America.)

Intermediate Level Questions

Encourage students at this level to offer verbal responses or short written responses to the following questions.

1. Look at Section 1. Why did the United States need more foreign trade? (The United States was producing more than it needed.)

2. Look at Section 1. Why did American planters in Hawaii want to control the government of Hawaii? (money)

3. Look at Section 2. What was the result of the explosion of the *Maine*? (The United States declared war on Spain.)

4. Look at Section 3. What agreement did the United States make with Panama to build the Panama Canal? (The United States helped Panama rebel against Colombia and paid Panama $10 million and $250,000 a year in rent on a right-of-way across the isthmus of Panama.)

5. Look at Section 3. What are two things that had to happen before the Panama Canal could be built? (The mosquitoes had to be eliminated, and sanitary conditions had to be improved.)

Advanced Level Questions

Encourage students at this level to provide written responses in complete sentences to the following questions.

1. Why is Pearl Harbor important? (It gave the United States a port for refueling and helped expand trade with Asia.)

2. Why did the United States become involved in a revolt against Queen Liliuokalani? (She was opposed to American power and the use of Pearl Harbor. American planters and traders feared they would lose a great deal of money.)

3. What did the United States gain in the Treaty of Paris? (The United States gained control of Cuba, Puerto Rico, the Philippines, and other islands in the Pacific.)

4. What two events during this time period made the United States a world power? (The two events that made the United States a world power were winning the Spanish-American War and building and controlling the Panama Canal.)

5. What did the Roosevelt Corollary allow the United States to do? (The Roosevelt Corollary gave the United States an excuse to interfere in the affairs of Latin American countries.)

Closing the Chapter

Ask students to look at the timeline they created for the Organizing Information activity on page 32 of this guide. Have students use the events in the part of the timeline that spans from 1890–1914 to help them write a summary about what they learned in the chapter.

Chapter 17 — World War I (1914–1920)

pages 308–329

▶ Introducing the Chapter

Tapping Prior Knowledge

Ask students to preview the chapter by reading the headings and subheadings and by looking at the art and photos (on pages 308, 313, 314, 315, 316, 318, 320, and 325 of the Student Edition), the timeline (on pages 308–309 of the Student Edition), the maps (on pages 312 and 326 of the Student Edition) and the chart (on page 324 of the Student Edition). Ask students to brainstorm what they already know about World War I. These could include reasons for why the war started, figures who played a major role in the war, and where the war took place. Then, ask students, *Why is it important to know the reasons why a war took place?*

Preteaching Vocabulary

Personalizing Vocabulary Begin by asking students to preview the chapter for five unfamiliar words or phrases and to record them in their Word Logs. Once students have identified these words and phrases, ask them to use their dictionaries to define them.

Identifying Essential Vocabulary Go over the pronunciation and meaning of each word and phrase in the box below. Then, ask students to work with a partner to write the sentence where they find the word in the chapter and then replace the word or phrase with a word with which they are familiar. Students may wish to consult their bilingual dictionaries as they rewrite the sentences.

Word or Phrase	Meaning
neutral	not choosing one side or another (p.311)
took cover	found a safe place to hide (p.312)
sneak up	surprise someone (p.316)
ocean liner	ship (p.316)
casualties	people who were hurt (p.322)
broke out	happened (p.322)
took power	took control of a situation (p.322)
convoy	a group of ships that are traveling together (p.323)

▶ Applying Content Knowledge

From the Chapter: Connecting History and Language (page 318)

Ask students to read Connecting History and Language: Propaganda on page 318. Ask students, *What do the words* fact, opinion, *and* propaganda *mean?* Encourage students to use their bilingual dictionaries to define the words. Work with students to help them understand the concept of propaganda. Ask students, *How do you know when something is propaganda?*

Using Visuals

Ask students to study the maps on pages 312 and 326 of the Student Edition and list the changes in Europe that resulted from the war. Then, ask students to list the new independent countries and the original country they were created from.

Summarizing

Ask students to choose one of the events of the war, such as the sinking of the *Lusitania*, the Zimmermann telegram, the air war, or one of the battles at Belleau Wood or Argonne Forest. Distribute the Outline on page 75 of this guide. Have students outline the story they choose and then write a summary using their completed outlines. Then, ask students to retell the story to a partner. If questions arise during the telling of the stories, encourage students to ask their partners about anything that was unclear.

Assessing Content Knowledge

Ask students to respond to the following questions. You may wish to encourage students with higher language proficiency to help beginning level students understand the questions.

Beginning Level Questions

Encourage students at this level to think about the answers to these questions and offer short verbal responses.

1. Look at page 311. What event started the war? (the assassination of Archduke Franz Ferdinand)

2. Look at page 311. What were the two sides in the war? (Central Powers and Allied Nations)

3. Look at pages 316–317. What two events helped the United States to enter the war? (the sinking of the *Lusitania* and the Zimmermann Telegram)

4. Look at page 319. What did the Selective Service Act do? (said that all men between the ages of 21 and 30 had to sign up for the draft)

5. Look at pages 323–324. What were two important battles the Americans fought? (Belleau Wood and Argonne Forest)

Intermediate Level Questions

Encourage students at this level to offer verbal responses or short written responses to the following questions.

1. Look at Section 1. Why was Archduke Franz Ferdinand assassinated? (A Serbian terrorist wanted Bosnia to be free from Austria.)

2. Look at Section 1. What countries were allied with each other? (the Central Powers: Germany, Austria-Hungary, and the Ottoman Empire; the Allies: Great Britain, France, and Russia)

3. Look at Section 2. What events caused the United States to stop being neutral? (sinking of the *Lusitania*, Zimmermann Telegram)

4. Look at Section 2. How did war bonds support the war? (Bonds provided money for the government to pay for the war.)

5. Look at Section 3. What happened in Russia that changed the war? (a revolution)

Advanced Level Questions

Encourage students at this level to provide written responses in complete sentences to the following questions.

1. What is the purpose of an alliance? (The purpose of an alliance is protection.)

2. Why did Wilson want the United States to remain neutral? (Wilson thought that by remaining neutral, he could help bring the Allies and the Central Powers together.)

3. Why was this war different from other wars? (Entire nations were involved in this war, and many civilians died.)

4. How was the U.S. economy changed by the war? (Women replaced men in jobs.)

5. Why was having America join the war so important in 1917? (Russia left the war.)

Closing the Chapter

Distribute the Timeline on page 72 of this guide. Ask students to make a timeline of the war, beginning with events leading up to the war and ending with the Treaty of Versailles. Then, ask students to use their timelines to write a summary about what they learned in the chapter.

Chapter 18
The Roaring Twenties (1920–1929)
pages 332–349

▶ Introducing the Chapter

Tapping Prior Knowledge

Ask students to preview the chapter by reading the headings and subheadings and by looking at the art and photos (on pages 331, 332, 336, 339, 341, and 345 of the Student Edition), the timeline (on pages 332–333 of the Student Edition), the numbered lists (on pages 335–336, 342–343, 344, and 346 of the Student Edition), and the charts (on pages 338 and 342 of the Student Edition). Ask students what the phrase *the Roaring Twenties* means. Have students suggest possible meanings of the phrase and work with students to arrive at a clear definition. Then, ask students, *What kind of a time does the Roaring Twenties sound like?*

Preteaching Vocabulary

Personalizing Vocabulary Begin by asking students to preview the chapter for five unfamiliar words or phrases and to record them in their Word Logs. Once students have identified these words and phrases, ask them to use their dictionaries to define them.

Identifying Essential Vocabulary Go over the pronunciation and meaning of each word and phrase in the box below. Then, distribute the three-column chart on page 74 of this guide. Ask students to write the headings **Positive, Neutral,** and **Negative** for the three columns. Ask students to classify each word and phrase as positive, neutral, or negative. Then, have students write a sentence using each word and phrase.

Word or Phrase	Meaning
prosperity	having money (p.334)
way of life	the way most people live (p.335)
scandal	bad behavior that causes embarrassment (p.335)
suburb	a place people live outside a city (p.336)
money down	to leave an amount of money (p.337)
the arts	music, movies, theater, and books (p.339)
racial pride	happiness with who someone is (p.341)

▶ Applying Content Knowledge

From the Chapter: History Fact (page 340)

Ask students to read the History Fact on page 340 of the Student Edition. Have students picture themselves sitting in front of a radio in order to receive information. Ask students to think about how election returns are announced today. Students' answers should include radio, newspapers, television, and the Internet. Ask students, *How is receiving information from the radio different from receiving it from a newspaper, television, or the Internet?*

Note-taking

Distribute copies of the Idea Web on page 76 of this guide. Use the chapter title, **The Roaring Twenties,** as the central topic. Place the headings **A Time of Prosperity, Good Times for Many,** and **A Time of Change** in the outer shapes. Then, ask students to list key details that they learned about each heading.

Organizing Information

Ask students to read Building Your Skills: Comparing on a Chart on page 338 of the Student Edition. Then, distribute the three-column chart on page 74 of this guide. Ask students to label the columns **Topic, Then: 1920s,** and **Now: The Year ____.** Ask students to work in groups to brainstorm a list of differences between the 1920s and present-day. You might wish to suggest these topics: clothing, entertainment, communication, or travel.

Then and Now		
Topic	Then: 1920s	Now: The Year ____
Clothing		
Entertainment		
Communication		
Travel		

Assessing Content Knowledge

Ask students to respond to the following questions. You may wish to encourage students with higher language proficiency to help beginning level students understand the questions.

Beginning Level Questions

Encourage students at this level to think about the answers to these questions and offer short verbal responses.

1. Look at page 335. What new jobs did the automobile create? (selling, repairing, parking, and driving cars)

2. Look at page 339. Why was the 1920s called the Jazz Age? (Jazz, a new kind of music, became popular.)

3. Look at page 341. What was the Harlem Renaissance? (a period in which African Americans used literature and art to show their racial pride and speak out against discrimination)

4. Look at page 342. What was the Nineteenth Amendment? (It gave all women the right to vote in all elections.)

5. Look at page 346. What was the Great Migration? (the migration of African Americans from the South to cities in the North)

Intermediate Level Questions

Encourage students at this level to offer verbal responses or short written responses to the following questions.

1. Look at Section 1. What was the scandal during President Harding's administration? (the Teapot Dome scandal)

2. Look at Section 1. How does an assembly line work? (Each worker does a different job. As parts are sent down the line, each person adds a part to the product. When the product reaches the end of the line, it is finished.)

3. Look at Section 2. Why was the Harlem Renaissance important? (African Americans were able to show their racial pride and speak out against racial discrimination through their art and literature.)

4. Look at Section 2. In the 1920s, how did young women show their independence? (They cut their hair short; wore short dresses, and began to speak out.)

5. Look at Section 3. In the 1920s, how did African Americans fight back against racism? (by forming groups that increased their racial pride)

Advanced Level Questions

Encourage students at this level to provide written responses in complete sentences to the following questions.

1. What was the Teapot Dome scandal? (It involved Albert Fall, the Secretary of the Interior, who accepted bribes from oil companies. He was found guilty and went to jail.)

2. Why was the assembly line important in changing the American way of life? (The assembly line allowed things to be made faster and cheaper.)

3. Why did having cars allow people to move out of the city? (More roads and cars meant people could travel longer distances to work.)

4. Why was entertainment important in the 1920s? (Answers will vary. Students' answers should include suggestions that the 1920s were a period of prosperity and that people had more leisure time.)

5. What discrimination against women still existed in the 1920s? (Women were not trained for some jobs; they were paid less than men; and many hospitals and law offices refused to hire women doctors and lawyers.)

Closing the Chapter

Ask students to use the Idea Web that they completed for the Note-taking activity on page 36 of the guide and the three-column chart that they completed for the Organizing Information activity on page 36 of this guide to write a summary of what they learned in the chapter.

Chapter 19 — The Great Depression (1929–1934)
pages 350–367

▶ Introducing the Chapter

Tapping Prior Knowledge
Ask students to preview the chapter by reading the headings and subheadings and by looking at the art and photos (on pages 350, 352, 354, 355, 360, 362, and 364 of the Student Edition), the timeline (on pages 350–351 of the Student Edition), the numbered lists (on pages 355 and 364 of the Student Edition), and the map (on page 358 of the Student Edition). Ask students if they ever heard of the Great Depression. Have students suggest possible meanings of the phrase and work with students to arrive at a definition. Then, ask students, *What does it mean for a country to be depressed?*

Preteaching Vocabulary
Personalizing Vocabulary Begin by asking students to preview the chapter for five unfamiliar words or phrases and to record them in their Word Logs. Once students have identified these words and phrases, ask them to use their dictionaries to define them.

Identifying Essential Vocabulary Go over the pronunciation and meaning of each word and phrase in the box below. Then, have students create a chart using the following headings: **Word or Phrase, Clues From the Text, Definition, How I Can Remember the Meaning,** and **My Sentence.** Students may choose to draw a picture or use a brief explanation in the **How I Can Remember the Meaning** column.

Word or Phrase	Meaning
installment plan	a way to pay a smaller amount of money over a period of time (p.352)
plunged	fell (p.353)
falls sharply	to go down quickly (p.353)
goods	items; things (p.354)
government charity	money that the government gives to people to help them (p.355)
sickened	made to not feel good (p.356)
ran errands	did certain tasks (p.357)

▶ Applying Content Knowledge

From the Chapter: Connecting History and the Environment (page 362)
Ask students to read Connecting History and the Environment: The Dust Bowl on page 362 of the Student Edition. Ask students what the phrase *the dust bowl* means. Encourage students to use context clues from Connecting History and the Environment: The Dust Bowl to try to define the phrase. Have students suggest possible meanings of the phrase and work with students to arrive at a clear explanation of the phrase. Then, distribute the Cause and Effect chart on page 80 of this guide. Have students work in small groups to show the causes leading to the creation of the Dust Bowl and the effects that the Dust Bowl had on the lives of Americans in the 1930s.

Using Visuals
Ask students to study the map on page 358 of the Student Edition. Ask students, *What states were most affected by the Dust Bowl? What states were least affected by the Dust Bowl?* Write students' answers on the chalkboard or ask students to record the answers on their own sheets of paper. After students finish compiling the list of states, ask them, *What are some possible reasons why the western states were not affected by the dust?*

Personalizing the Lesson
Ask students to read A Closer Look: Teenagers in the Great Depression on page 354 of the Student Edition. Then, distribute the Venn diagram on page 77 of this guide. Ask students to label the sections **Lives of Teenagers in the Great Depression, Both,** and **Lives of Teenagers Today.** Then, have students use their Venn diagrams to compare and contrast the lives of teenagers in the Great Depression to the lives of teenagers today.

Assessing Content Knowledge

Ask students to respond to the following questions. You may wish to encourage students with higher language proficiency to help beginning level students understand the questions.

Beginning Level Questions
Encourage students at this level to think about the answers to these questions and offer short verbal responses.

1. Look at the Economics Fact on page 353. What was Black Tuesday? (the day the N.Y. Stock Market crashed)

2. Look at pages 353–354. What happened to farmers when the depression began? (Farmers lost farms.)

3. Look at page 357. What are three ways that the Great Depression changed American families? (Some grew closer; some were torn apart; many men left their wives and children; many teenagers left home; and many young children had to work to help their families survive.)

4. Look at page 359. What kind of hardship did the Great Depression have on African Americans? (African Americans became poorer and couldn't find jobs.)

5. Look at page 364. What laws did President Hoover create to help Americans? (started public works; cut taxes; and lent money to banks and businesses)

Intermediate Level Questions
Encourage students at this level to offer verbal responses or short written responses to the following questions.

1. Look at Section 1. How did buying stocks in the 1920s help people make money? (They became part owners in businesses when they bought stock. As the businesses grew, they would make money.)

2. Look at Section 1. Why did the United States enter a depression in the 1920s? (The stock market crashed.)

3. Look at Section 2. How did the Great Depression affect Mexican Americans and Mexican immigrants? (They faced discrimination and poverty.)

4. Look at Section 3. What did President Hoover do to help the American people during the Depression? (He asked Congress to pass several laws.)

5. Look at Section 3. How did Franklin Roosevelt feel about the government helping Americans? (He felt it was the government's responsibility to end the depression.)

Advanced Level Questions
Encourage students at this level to provide written responses in complete sentences to the following questions.

1. Why did people that bought stocks in the 1920s lose money? (They bought stocks on borrowed money. When the stock prices fell, they lost money and then could not repay what they borrowed.)

2. Why did banks foreclose on farmers' properties? (When farmers began to default on their payments to the bank, the banks foreclosed on their properties.)

3. How did Americans react when government and big business failed to help them during the Great Depression? (Americans reacted in the following four ways: Some people joined the Communist party; some farmers destroyed their crops; some farmers joined together to stop banks from taking their property; and many World War I veterans marched on Washington, D.C., in 1932.)

4. Why was the Dust Bowl region difficult for farmers? (A drought turned the Great Plains into dusty, dry land that could no longer be farmed.)

5. What is the difference between President Hoover's and Franklin Roosevelt's feelings about the government helping Americans? (President Hoover felt Americans should help themselves, and Franklin Roosevelt felt it was the government's responsibility.)

Closing the Chapter

Ask students to use the timeline on pages 350–351 of the Student Edition to summarize what they learned in the chapter.

The New Deal (1933–1941)

pages 368–385

▶ Introducing the Chapter

Tapping Prior Knowledge

Ask students to preview the chapter by reading the headings and subheadings and by looking at the art and photos (on pages 368, 371, 372, 374, 378, 380, 381, and 382 of the Student Edition), the timeline (on pages 368–369 of the Student Edition), the numbered lists (on pages 371, 375, 376, and 378–379 of the Student Edition), and the charts (on pages 373 and 377 of the Student Edition). Then, direct students to the chart on page 377. Ask students, *How much should a government do to help a country? When should the government get involved? Why was it important for Roosevelt and his government to help the American people during the Great Depression?*

Preteaching Vocabulary

Personalizing Vocabulary Begin by asking students to preview the chapter for five unfamiliar words or phrases and to record them in their Word Logs. Once students have identified these words and phrases, ask them to use their dictionaries to define them.

Identifying Essential Vocabulary Go over the pronunciation and meaning of each word and phrase in the box below. Then, model the words and phrases in the box below by saying the following sentence: *Even though Matt* stood for *a lot of good things, many people accused him of* packing *the election since he won by a* landslide. Ask students to have a brief conversation using the words and phrases from the box.

Word or Phrase	Meaning
landslide	to win by getting a lot of votes (p.370)
stood for	things people believed in (p.371)
put his plans into action	to cause something to happen (p.372)
packing	to arrange things to one's advantage or to suit one's purpose (p.377)
role	part; function (p.378)

▶ Applying Content Knowledge

From the Chapter: Great Names in History (page 378)

Ask students to read Great Names in History: Eleanor Roosevelt on page 378 of the Student Edition. Discuss with students all of the things that Eleanor Roosevelt did while she was first lady. Ask students, *Why do you think that Eleanor Roosevelt was one of the most active reformers ever to live in the White House?*

Organizing Information

Distribute the KWL chart on page 79 of this guide. Before you begin to study each section, allow students to complete the **K** and the **W** columns of the chart for that section. Before beginning each section, ask students, *What would you like to learn in this section?* Have students complete the **L** column of the chart once they have completed each section of the chapter.

Using Manipulatives

Ask students to work in pairs to write events that influenced the end of the Great Depression in chronological order. Have the students cut the list into strips, rearrange the order of events, and exchange with other pairs of students to sequence.

Personalizing the Lesson

Ask students to read President Franklin D. Roosevelt's comments from Voices From The Past: Franklin D. Roosevelt on page 374 of the Student Edition. Ask students, *Why might people find Roosevelt's words inspirational?* Ask students what the word *inspirational* means. Encourage students to use their bilingual dictionaries to define the word. Then, ask students to write a paragraph stating how his words could serve as an inspiration.

▶ Assessing Content Knowledge

Ask students to respond to the following questions. You may wish to encourage students with higher language proficiency to help beginning level students understand the questions.

Beginning Level Questions

Encourage students at this level to think about the answers to these questions and offer short verbal responses.

1. Look at page 370. Who became President of the United States in the election of 1932? (Roosevelt)

2. Look at page 371. What did the Three R's stand for in President Roosevelt's New Deal? (relief, recovery, and reform)

3. Look at pages 370–372. What are three ways that President Roosevelt tried to end the depression? (developed New Deal Plan, created Brain Trust, had fireside chats, created programs for social reform, increased the Supreme Court, and proposed new laws)

4. Look at page 376. What are two reasons why liberals did not like Roosevelt's New Deal? (See page 376.)

5. Look at page 383. What is anti-Semitism? (the practice of hating Jewish people because they are Jewish)

Intermediate Level Questions

Encourage students at this level to offer verbal responses or short written responses to the following questions.

1. Look at Section 1. Why was Franklin D. Roosevelt a popular President? (He promised to help the U.S. economy.)

2. Look at Section 1. What were fireside chats? (radio communication with President Roosevelt and Americans)

3. Look at Section 1. How did the new programs created by the New Deal help Americans? (The programs created new jobs and agencies for social reform that also increased jobs for women and minorities.)

4. Look at Section 2. What were the reasons some people did not like President Roosevelt's New Deal? (It raised business taxes; interfered too much in people's lives; spent too much money; was not strong enough to solve the problems, and was more of the same old ideas.)

5. Look at Section 3. Why was Jesse Owens an important figure in the 1936 Summer Olympics? (He won four medals and the favor of the German people.)

Advanced Level Questions

Encourage students at this level to provide written responses in complete sentences to the following questions.

1. Why was Roosevelt's New Deal important to Americans? (The New Deal gave hope for an end to the depression. It was supposed to change laws so people could have jobs again.)

2. Why was the Brain Trust valuable for Frances Perkins, other women, and minorities? (Frances Perkins was the first female Cabinet member. The Brain Trust gave opportunities for women and minorities to be involved in public decisions.)

3. How did President Roosevelt's new laws and programs affect women and minorities? (Women became involved in political positions, some African Americans became advisers to President Roosevelt, and Native Americans were allowed to return to their land and way of life.)

4. How did President Roosevelt's actions influence the Supreme Court? (He thought that the country needed more and younger judges.)

5. Why were movies, radio, sporting events, and books popular during the depression? (People wanted to forget for a short time about how hard their lives were, so they used different kinds of entertainment.)

▶ Closing the Chapter

Ask students to use the KWL charts they completed for the Organizing Information activity on page 40 of this guide to write a summary about what they learned.

Chapter 21 / Leading Up to War (1922–1941)

pages 388–403

▶ Introducing the Chapter

Tapping Prior Knowledge

Ask students to preview the chapter by reading the headings and subheadings and by looking at the art and photos (on pages 387, 388, 391, 392, and 398 of the Student Edition), the timeline (on pages 388–389 of the Student Edition), the map (on page 393 of the Student Edition), and the chart (on page 400 of the Student Edition). Ask students what the phrase *national pride* means. Encourage students to use their bilingual dictionaries to define any words in the expression that may be unfamiliar. Have students suggest possible meanings of the phrase and work with students to arrive at a clear definition. Then, ask students, *When is national pride not a good thing?*

Preteaching Vocabulary

Personalizing Vocabulary Begin by asking students to preview the chapter for five unfamiliar words or phrases and to record them in their Word Logs. Once students have identified these words and phrases, ask them to use their dictionaries to define them.

Identifying Essential Vocabulary Go over the pronunciation and meaning of each word and phrase in the box below. Then, ask each student to write a sentence for each word. Have students rewrite their sentences leaving a blank space in place of the vocabulary term. Have students trade sentences with a partner and fill in the blanks in the sentences their partner wrote.

Word or Phrase	Meaning
crisis	emergency (p.387)
drawn into	became involved in (p.389)
torn apart	in a state of disorder; a mess (p.390)
weakened	to make less strong (p.391)
prime minister	the head of a country (p.391)
hand over	give (p.393)
run for	take part; participate; be involved (p.399)
ally	friend; partner (p.400)

▶ Applying Content Knowledge

From the Chapter: Building Your Skills (page 395)

Ask students to read the feature entitled Building Your Skills: Recognizing a Point of View on page 395 of the Student Edition. Divide students into two groups: Isolationist and Involvement. Ask students in the Isolationist group to look through the chapter and identify efforts and reasons to stay out of the war, and ask students in the Involvement group to look through the chapter and identify efforts and reasons to enter the war. Ask both groups to present their positions in a panel discussion, a debate, or by role-playing as concerned citizens.

Organizing Information

Distribute the Who, What, Why, Where, When, and How chart on page 81 of this guide. Ask students to work with a partner and complete a chart for each of the three sections of the chapter. Students may wish to write **Who Was Involved** underneath the word **Who** in the chart, **What Happened** underneath the word **What** in the chart, **Where It Happened** underneath the word **Where** in the chart, **When It Happened** underneath the word **When** in the chart, **Why It Happened** underneath the word **Why** in the chart, and **How It Happened** underneath the word **How** in the chart. Have students complete their charts as they read the chapter.

Summarizing

Direct students to the heading The Road to War on page 392 of the Student Edition and War Breaks Out Again on page 394 of the Student Edition. Distribute the Sequence of Events chart on page 71 of this guide. Ask students to work in pairs to sequence five steps that show that Germany wanted to control Europe. You may wish to ask students to summarize their steps in a single paragraph.

Assessing Content Knowledge

Ask students to respond to the following questions. You may wish to encourage students with higher language proficiency to help beginning level students understand the questions.

Beginning Level Questions

Encourage students at this level to think about the answers to these questions and offer short verbal responses.

1. Look at pages 391–392. Who were the three dictators in major European countries in the 1920s and 1930s? (Stalin, Hitler, and Mussolini)

2. Look at page 392. Who did Hitler blame for Germany's problems? (Jews and Communists)

3. Look at page 397. What did Japan want to control? (all of eastern Asia)

4. Look at the poster on page 398. What is its purpose? (to encourage the United States to stay out of the war)

5. Look at page 401. What happened at Pearl Harbor? (The Japanese attacked, killing more than 2,400 Americans.)

Intermediate Level Questions

Encourage students at this level to offer verbal responses or short written responses to the following questions.

1. Look at Section 1. What countries were controlled by totalitarian governments? (Russia, Germany, Italy)

2. Look at Section 1. What did Hitler believe about Germans? (that they were the master race and should rule the world)

3. Look at Section 1. Why did the United States want to help Great Britain in the war? (It was afraid Hitler would want to take over the Western Hemisphere.)

4. Look at Section 2. Why did Japan sign an anti-Communist agreement with Germany and Italy? (to become a world power with Germany and Italy)

5. Look at Section 3. Why did the Japanese attack Pearl Harbor? (They felt it would take the United States a while to rebuild its forces after the attack.)

Advanced Level Questions

Encourage students at this level to provide written responses in complete sentences to the following questions.

1. What happened to people who spoke out against their totalitarian governments? (They were arrested, beaten, or killed.)

2. What was Hitler's goal for Germany? (He wanted Germany to become the most powerful country in the world.)

3. What was Japan's goal? (Japan wanted to control eastern Asia and become a world power.)

4. What did the United States do to make Germany and Japan angry? (It adopted the Lend-Lease plan and banned oil shipments to Japan.)

5. What was the United States' response to the attack on Pearl Harbor? (Congress declared war on Japan.)

Closing the Chapter

Ask students to use the Who, What, Why, Where, When, and How charts that they completed for the Organizing Information activity on page 42 of this guide to write a summary about what they learned in the chapter.

Chapter 22 — A World at War (1941–1945)

Introducing the Chapter

Tapping Prior Knowledge

Ask students to preview the chapter by reading the headings and subheadings and by looking at the art and photos (on pages 404, 407, 410, 414, 415, 416, 419, and 422 of the Student Edition), the timeline (on pages 404–405 of the Student Edition), the map (on page 411 of the Student Edition), and the numbered lists (on pages 413 and 416 of the Student Edition). Then, ask students to tell what they know about World War II. Ask students, *Why is it important to know the causes of a war?* Students should suggest that knowing the causes of a war could keep history from repeating itself. Ask students, *How can knowing the causes of a war help an entire world?*

Preteaching Vocabulary

Personalizing Vocabulary Begin by asking students to preview the chapter for five unfamiliar words or phrases and to record them in their Word Logs. Once students have identified these words and phrases, ask them to use their dictionaries to define them.

Identifying Essential Vocabulary Go over the pronunciation and meaning of each word and phrase in the box below. Then, provide sheets of graph paper with large boxes and ask students to use the words and phrases to create a crossword puzzle. Have students use sentences from the text as clues.

Word or Phrase	Meaning
turned against	was opposed to (p.409)
code	secret language (p.411)
coupon	a piece of paper used to buy something (p.414)
defense plant	factory that made war supplies (p.416)
armed forces	a nation's military troops (p.416)
highly decorated	receiving many awards, medals, and honors (p.418)

Applying Content Knowledge

From the Chapter: A Closer Look (page 410)

Ask students to read A Closer Look: Navajo Code Talkers on page 410 of the Student Edition. Ask students to think about times when they wanted to tell someone something, but they did not want another person to understand it. Ask students, *Why were the Navajo Code Talkers important in the war?*

Organizing Information

Distribute the Idea Web on page 76 of this guide. As students read the chapter, ask them to fill in the Idea Web. Use the chapter title, **A World at War**, as the central topic. Place the headings **A World at War Again**, **The Allies Strike Back**, **The War at Home**, and **Winning the War** in the outer shapes. Then, ask students to list key details that they learned about each heading.

Summarizing

Write these headlines on the chalkboard: GERMAN ARMY ATTACKS POLAND; CITIES BOMBED, PORT BLOCKADED; U.S. AT WAR! Tell students that these are headlines from U.S. newspapers during World War II. Divide the class into three groups, one to cover events in Europe, one to cover events in the United States, and one to cover events in Asia. Ask each group to write a headline and paragraph about the events in its area during the war. You may wish to distribute the Who, What, Why, Where, When, and How chart on page 81 of this guide to help students construct their paragraphs.

Assessing Content Knowledge

Ask students to respond to the following questions. You may wish to encourage students with higher language proficiency to help beginning level students understand the questions.

Beginning Level Questions

Encourage students at this level to think about the answers to these questions and offer short verbal responses.

1. Look at page 407. What was the Bataan Death March? (the 65-mile journey by Americans and Filipinos to the prison camps)

2. Look at page 408. Who were the Big Three Allied leaders? (Roosevelt, Churchill, and Stalin)

3. Look at the map on page 411. Where did the Japanese and the Allies have major battles? (Leyte Gulf; Okinawa; Iwo Jima; Guadalcanal; Tarawa; Midway Island; and Pearl Harbor)

4. Look at the poster and its caption on page 416. Why was it important? (Answers will vary. Students' answers should include ideas about encouraging people, supporting women in the war effort, and promoting a strong war effort at home.)

5. Look at page 417. How many Latinos served in the armed forces? (more than 300,000)

Intermediate Level Questions

Encourage students at this level to offer verbal responses or short written responses to the following questions.

1. Look at Section 1. What was the Allies' plan for winning the war? (They decided to attack North Africa first. Then, they would attack the west coast of Europe and finally the Pacific area.)

2. Look at Section 2. What did island-hopping mean? (It referred to Marines who made amphibious landings on certain islands in the Pacific.)

3. Look at Section 3. What are four new responsibilities that women had during the war? (Women served in the armed forces, worked in military offices, flew supply planes, and served as nurses.)

4. Look at Section 3. Who were the Tuskegee Airmen? (African American fighter pilots)

5. Look at Section 4. What was D-Day? (the day of the Allied invasion of Europe)

Advanced Level Questions

Encourage students at this level to provide written responses in complete sentences to the following questions.

1. Why was the defeat of Rommel important to the war? (Answers will vary. Students' answers should include that it was the first step in the plan to defeat Germany, and it gave the Allies entry into Italy.)

2. What were the partisans in Italy? (Partisans were Italians who were fighting the Fascists and Nazis.)

3. How did code-breaking help the Allies defeat Japan? (Navy code experts were able to figure out the secret messages being sent between Japanese ships, so U.S. ships always knew where the enemy ships were going to be.)

4. How did the war change women's lives? (Women became workers; they had a new sense of freedom; and they served in the armed forces.)

5. Why is the 442nd Infantry important? (The 442nd Infantry was important because it contained a Japanese American unit that was highly decorated.)

Closing the Chapter

Ask students to use the Idea Web that they completed for the Organizing Information activity on page 44 of this guide to write a summary about what they learned in the chapter.

Chapter 23 The Cold War (1945–1960) pages 426–443

▶ Introducing the Chapter

Tapping Prior Knowledge

Ask students to preview the chapter by reading the headings and subheadings and by looking at the art and photos (on pages 426, 431, 434, 436, 439, and 440 of the Student Edition), the timeline (on pages 426–427 of the Student Edition), the numbered list (on page 431 of Student Edition), and the map (on page 432 of the Student Edition). Tell students that much of this unit is about communism. Encourage students to discuss their experiences or the experiences of people they know on the subject of communism. Ask students, *Why do you suppose the United States was so afraid of the spread of communism in the world?*

Preteaching Vocabulary

Personalizing Vocabulary Begin by asking students to preview the chapter for five unfamiliar words or phrases and to record them in their Word Logs. Once students have identified these words and phrases, ask them to use their dictionaries to define them.

Identifying Essential Vocabulary Go over the pronunciation and meaning of each word and phrase in the box below. Then, ask students to work with a partner to find the words and phrases in the box below as they are used in the text. Ask students to list the words (context clues) in the sentence or paragraph that help them to understand the word.

Word or Phrase	Meaning
tight grip	to hold firmly (p.429)
showdown	fight (p.430)
military advisers	people who give their suggestions about issues of war (p.430)
carry out	do (p.434)
testify	to say something is true in court (p.438)
atomic weapon	a nuclear bomb (p.440)
radioactive waste	the material that is left over when a nuclear bomb explodes (p.440)

▶ Applying Content Knowledge

From the Chapter: Connecting History and Government (page 434)

Ask students to read Connecting History and Government: The United Nations on page 434 of the Student Edition. Then, have students work in groups and write five questions and answers. Ask students to play a group Q & A game. One group asks a question and chooses another group to answer the question. The group that answers will ask the next question.

Note-taking

Ask students to read A New Kind of War and The Truman Doctrine on pages 429–430. Then, ask students to work in small groups to find four statements of fact and four opinions. Remind students that facts can be checked or proven, whereas opinions are beliefs, feelings, or attitudes. You might wish to suggest that students review Distinguishing Fact From Opinion on page 221 of the Student Edition.

Organizing Information

Distribute the Main Idea and Supporting Details chart on page 78 of this guide. Ask students to read A Closer Look: The Space Race on page 440 of the Student Edition. Then, ask students to complete a Main Idea and Supporting Details chart for each paragraph. Have students use their completed charts to summarize the information for a partner.

Personalizing the Lesson

Ask students what the phrase *Cold War* means. Encourage students to use their bilingual dictionaries to define any words in the expression that may be unfamiliar. Have students suggest possible meanings of the phrase and work with students to arrive at a clear explanation of the phrase. Then, tell students that many people in the world were very afraid of nuclear weapons in the 1950s. Ask students to interview their family members, friends, or other people who recall the 1950s. Have students ask what they remember about the Cold War and how it affected their lives. You might wish to ask students to share their stories with the class or write them in a paragraph for inclusion in a class notebook.

Assessing Content Knowledge

Ask students to respond to the following questions. You may wish to encourage students with higher language proficiency to help beginning level students understand the questions.

Beginning Level Questions

Encourage students at this level to think about the answers to these questions and offer short verbal responses.

1. Look at the History Fact on page 429. Who gave the famous Iron Curtain Speech? (Winston Churchill)

2. Look at the map on page 432. Which countries did not belong to NATO or to the Warsaw Pact? (Ireland; Spain; Switzerland; Austria; Sweden; Finland; and Yugoslavia)

3. Look at page 433. What is NATO? (North Atlantic Treaty Organization, which consisted of the United States, Canada, and 10 countries that signed a treaty that said if a member nation were attacked, all other member nations would help that nation)

4. Look at page 437. In June 1950, who attacked South Korea? (North Korean troops)

5. Look at page 439. What was McCarthyism? (accusing people of being Communists)

Intermediate Level Questions

Encourage students at this level to offer verbal responses or short written responses to the following questions.

1. Look at Section 1. How did the Soviet Union control countries? (Secret police watched and listened everywhere; people were not allowed to speak out against their own governments; few people were allowed in or out of their countries; and people were not able to get news about the outside world.)

2. Look at Section 1. What was the Marshall Plan? (a plan to help Europeans rebuild their countries)

3. Look at Section 2. How was the Korean War resolved? (Both sides agreed to set up a demilitarized zone.)

4. Look at Section 3. What happened to some people who appeared before the House Un-American Activities Committee? (They were questioned and blacklisted, and their careers were ruined.)

5. Look at Section 3. Who was involved in the space race? (the United States and the Soviet Union)

Advanced Level Questions

Encourage students at this level to provide written responses in complete sentences to the following questions.

1. What was the difference in the way the United States and the Soviet Union treated countries after the war? (The United States held free elections. The Soviet Union used force to set up communist governments and made the countries satellites of the Soviet Union.)

2. What was the purpose of the Security Council of the United Nations? (It carries out actions against nations.)

3. What was the cause of the Korean War? (North Korean troops attacked South Korea hoping to unite the two under communism. President Truman and the United Nations sent troops to support South Korea.)

4. Why is atomic weapons testing dangerous? (The radioactive fallout can damage the environment.)

5. Why was NASA formed? (It was formed to control the U.S. space program because Americans feared the Soviets were ahead of the United States in the space race.)

Closing the Chapter

Ask students to summarize the most important points from the chapter by choosing the three most important events in the chapter and explaining them to a partner. Then, ask students to select one of the events they chose and write a paragraph to explain why they believe that it was the most important event.

Chapter 24 — Changing Ways of Life (1945–1960)
pages 446–463

▶ Introducing the Chapter

Tapping Prior Knowledge

Ask students to preview the chapter by reading the headings and subheadings and by looking at the art and photos (on pages 445, 446, 449, 450, 451, 452, and 458 of the Student Edition), the timeline (on pages 446–447 of the Student Edition), the numbered lists (on pages 448 and 449 of the Student Edition), and the charts (on pages 454 and 456 of the Student Edition). Ask students to think about what the world was like before television. Ask students, *How do you suppose television changed American life in the Fifties?*

Preteaching Vocabulary

Personalizing Vocabulary Begin by asking students to preview the chapter for five unfamiliar words or phrases and to record them in their Word Logs. Once students have identified these words and phrases, ask them to use their dictionaries to define them.

Identifying Essential Vocabulary Go over the pronunciation and meaning of each word and phrase in the box below. Then, ask students to create their own sentences for the words and phrases in the box below. Ask students to rewrite their sentences leaving a blank space for the word or phrase. Then, have students exchange sentences and fill in the blanks.

Word or Phrase	Meaning
in favor of	supports (p.448)
buying habits	how and what people purchase when they shop (p.457)
reached	got to (p.457)
disc jockey	a person who plays music on the radio (p.457)
role model	a person who is an example for others (p.458)
taste	what a person likes or prefers (p.458)
value	what a person believes is right or wrong (p.458)

▶ Applying Content Knowledge

From the Chapter: Building Your Skills (page 454)

Ask students to read Building Your Skills: Reading a Graph on page 454 of the Student Edition. Distribute the Who, What, Why, Where, When, and How chart on page 81 of this guide. Have students work with a partner to write six questions (who, what, why, where, when, and how), using the information in the graph. You might also wish to ask students to create their own graphs about their classmates using such topics as age, time spent watching TV, and daily class attendance.

Using Manipulatives

Ask students to make a poster using magazine cutouts and Internet photos to illustrate changes in teenagers' lives during the 1950s. Suggest that students provide both general and specific labels for their poster, such as *general: music; specific: Elvis, song titles, guitars, dances,* and so on. After students complete their posters, you may wish to ask students to share their posters with the rest of the class. Ask students, *Why did you choose the photos you chose?*

Using Visuals

Ask students to study the photos on pages 446, 450, and 451 of the Student Edition. Distribute the KWL chart on page 79 of this guide. Ask students to complete the **K** and the **W** columns of the chart based on the photographs. As students complete the **K** and the **W** columns, ask students to think about what they can tell about Americans' lives in the 1950s from the photographs.

Personalizing the Lesson

Ask students to choose one thing they like about the 1950s and discuss it with classmates.

Assessing Content Knowledge

Ask students to respond to the following questions. You may wish to encourage students with higher language proficiency to help beginning level students understand the questions.

Beginning Level Questions
Encourage students at this level to think about the answers to these questions and offer short verbal responses.

1. Look at page 448. What was the GI Bill of Rights? (an act passed to help soldiers who had fought in the war)

2. Look at page 450. What changes happened in the workplace? (automation, kind of work, jobs held by women)

3. Look at the graph on page 456. How many homes had TVs in 1950? In 1960? (4 million; 45 million)

4. Look at page 459. What was the Twenty-second Amendment to the Constitution? (It limited Presidents to two terms in office.)

5. Look at page 461. In 1959, in which country did communism take power? (Cuba)

Intermediate Level Questions
Encourage students at this level to offer verbal responses or short written responses to the following questions.

1. Look at Section 1. What did the GI Bill of Rights provide? (The GI Bill of Rights provided unemployment pay for one year to each veteran unable to find a job; special loans to buy houses or farms, or to start a business; and $500 a year to pay for a college education, plus money for rent and food.)

2. Look at Section 1. What were the results of automation? (more production with fewer work hours)

3. Look at Section 2. What things did TV change in the United States? (family life, politics, and buying habits)

4. Look at Section 3. Why was the Twenty-second Amendment to the Constitution passed? (Roosevelt was elected four times, breaking the precedent set by Washington that a President should serve only two terms.)

5. How did the interstate highway system change life in the United States? (People were able to drive across the country without stopping for traffic lights.)

Advanced Level Questions
Encourage students at this level to provide written responses in complete sentences to the following questions.

1. How did the GI Bill of Rights benefit the country? (The money improved the economy; educated GIs; helped to start businesses; and was used by GIs to buy real estate.)

2. Why did many women leave the workforce after the war? (Men returning from war had first chance at jobs; government, business, and unions wanted women to stay at home.)

3. How did TV affect U.S. politics? (Politicians were able to communicate to large numbers of people; the way politicians looked and sounded became important; it allowed politicians with the most money to buy the most time/ads.)

4. Why was the United States called a society of consumers? (Everywhere Americans looked, there were ads in magazines, in newspapers, on billboards, and on television encouraging them to buy more.)

5. What were some of Eisenhower's accomplishments as President? (Eisenhower approved the building of public housing in poor city neighborhoods; he created the Department of Health, Education, and Welfare; and he sponsored a law to create the interstate highway system.)

Closing the Chapter

Ask students to complete the L column of the KWL chart they began in the Using Visuals activity on page 48 of this guide. Then, ask students to use their completed charts to write a summary about what they learned in the chapter.

Chapter 25 / The Struggle for Equality (1947–1965)

pages 464–483

▶ Introducing the Chapter

Tapping Prior Knowledge

Ask students to preview the chapter by reading the headings and subheadings and by looking at the art and photos (on pages 464, 468, 471, 472, 474, 476, 479, and 481 of the Student Edition), the timeline (on pages 464–465 of the Student Edition), the map (on page 470 of the Student Edition), and the numbered lists (on pages 471–472, 475, and 478 of the Student Edition). Ask students what the concepts *civil rights* and *equality* mean. Have students suggest possible meanings and work with students to arrive at clear explanations. Then, discuss the concepts of civil rights and equality with students. Ask students, *How did the struggle for equal rights affect the United States?*

Preteaching Vocabulary

Personalizing Vocabulary Begin by asking students to preview the chapter for five unfamiliar words or phrases and to record them in their Word Logs. Once students have identified these words and phrases, ask them to use their dictionaries to define them.

Identifying Essential Vocabulary Go over the pronunciation and meaning of each word and phrase in the box below. Then, have the students create a chart using the following headings: **Word or Phrase, Clues From the Text, Definition, How I Can Remember the Meaning,** and **My Sentence.** Students may choose to draw a picture or use a brief explanation for **How I Can Remember the Meaning.**

Word or Phrase	Meaning
civil right	a right a person has because he or she is a part of a society (p.466)
segregated	separated (p.466)
sue	take to court (p.470)
review the decision	look over what was decided (p.470)
argue the case	debate the points of a lawsuit (p.471)
hate groups	people who dislike other people because of who they are (p.479)

▶ Applying Content Knowledge

From the Chapter: Voices From the Past (page 481)

Ask students to read Voices From the Past: Dr. Martin Luther King, Jr. on page 481 of the Student Edition. Ask students to research Dr. King's life and select five events when he promoted or served African American equality. You might also wish to ask students to note how each event worked toward a solution for the problem of inequality.

Organizing Information

Distribute the Outline on page 75 of this guide. As students read the chapter, ask them to use the outline to fill in the headings and corresponding details.

```
Topic: The Struggle for Equality
   I. Early Gains for Equal Rights
      A.
      B.
  II. Fighting for an Equal Education
      A.
      B.
 III. Protests and Marches for Equality
      A.
      B.
```

Using Resources

Ask students to read Dr. King's "I Have a Dream" speech. This may be found on the Internet or in the school library. Have students illustrate the main ideas with drawings, pictures, magazine cutouts, and symbols. You might also wish to ask students to explain their illustrations to the class.

Personalizing the Lesson

Ask students to look at the pictures of people engaged in protest on pages 472, 474, 476, and 479 and to think of the situations the protesters faced. Then, have students suppose that they wanted to protest a decision or action in their school, community, or country. Ask students, *What would you be willing to do to protest an action? Not willing to do?*

Assessing Content Knowledge

Ask students to respond to the following questions. You may wish to encourage students with higher language proficiency to help beginning level students understand the questions.

Beginning Level Questions

Encourage students at this level to think about the answers to these questions and offer short verbal responses.

1. Look at page 466. What was *Plessy* v. *Ferguson*? (a court case about separate railroad cars for African Americans and white people)

2. Look at page 467. What announcement did the Defense Department make in 1954? (There were not going to be any African American units in the armed forces.)

3. Look at the map on page 470. How many states had no segregation law? (11)

4. Look at page 474. Why was Rosa Parks arrested? (for refusing to give her seat to a white passenger)

5. Look at page 478. What three things did the Civil Rights Act do? (See page 478.)

Intermediate Level Questions

Encourage students at this level to offer verbal responses or short written responses to the following questions.

1. Look at Section 1. What was the difference in the treatment of African Americans in the North and in the South? (The South had Jim Crow laws.)

2. Look at Section 1. How were the armed forces integrated? (by an executive order)

3. Look at Section 2. What was school like for African American students? (Many African American children had to walk miles to their schools; they had to share books; the teachers were poorly trained; and the classes were overcrowded.)

4. Look at Section 3. After Rosa Parks was arrested, what three demands did Dr. Martin Luther King, Jr., present to the bus company? (See page 475.)

5. Look at Section 3. What did the Voting Rights Act of 1965 say? (States could not prevent African Americans from registering to vote.)

Advanced Level Questions

Encourage students at this level to provide written responses in complete sentences to the following questions.

1. Why did southern whites feel that the Jim Crow laws were legal? (A U.S. Supreme Court decision had supported separate but equal treatment of African Americans.)

2. What did the executive order signed by President Truman to integrate the armed forces say? (All jobs in the armed forces were opened to African Americans, units were integrated, and African American officers could command white soldiers.)

3. Why was the *Brown* v. *Board of Education of Topeka* decision important? (It said that "separate but equal" has no place in public schools.)

4. What was the Montgomery bus boycott? (African Americans refused to ride buses in Montgomery, Alabama. They walked or got rides until their demands were met.)

5. In what ways are nonviolent protests successful? (Answers will vary.)

Closing the Chapter

Ask students to use the Outline they completed for the Organizing Information activity on page 50 of this guide to summarize what they learned in the chapter.

Chapter 26
A New Frontier and a Great Society (1960–1968)
pages 484–501

▶ Introducing the Chapter

Tapping Prior Knowledge

Ask students to preview the chapter by reading the headings and subheadings and by looking at the art and photos (on pages 484, 487, 489, 491, 493, 494, and 497 of the Student Edition), the timeline (on pages 484–485 of the Student Edition), the map (on page 488 of the Student Edition), the numbered lists (on pages 489–490 and 497 of the Student Edition), and the chart (on page 498 of the Student Edition). Ask students to look at the quote from John F. Kennedy on page 488 of the Student Edition. Have students suggest possible meanings of the quote and work with students to arrive at a clear explanation of the quote. Ask students, *What message did President Kennedy's quote send to the American people?*

Preteaching Vocabulary

Personalizing Vocabulary Begin by asking students to preview the chapter for five unfamiliar words or phrases and to record them in their Word Logs. Once students have identified these words and phrases, ask them to use their dictionaries to define them.

Identifying Essential Vocabulary Go over the pronunciation and meaning of each word and phrase in the box below. Then, distribute an index card to each student. Ask each student to write a question on the index card using one or more of the vocabulary words. Then, have students select a partner to exchange cards with and have each student answer their partner's question.

Word or Phrase	Meaning
candidate	a person who is trying to get elected (p.486)
to run	to try to get elected (p.486)
cut off from	separated (p.494)
second term	four more years as President (p.495)
policies	plans (p.496)
elderly	older (p.497)
federal funding	paid for by the government (p.498)

▶ Applying Content Knowledge

From the Chapter: Citizenship Link (page 489)

Ask students to read Citizenship Link: Becoming a Volunteer on page 489 of the Student Edition. Remind students that the Kennedy years were a time when many young people became involved in government and in volunteering. Ask students to share times when they have volunteered to help others. Then, ask students to work in groups to research volunteer opportunities that young people, school clubs, or groups might find in their community. Have each group create a list of the opportunities they find.

Organizing Information

Distribute the Sequence of Events chart on page 71 of this guide. Ask students to work in groups to sequence 5 to 7 events that they learned about in the chapter. Suggest that they use the headings as guides. Possible choices might be: John F. Kennedy is elected President (3); Nixon and Kennedy debate their ideas on television (2); Kennedy is chosen by the Democrats to run for President (1); President Kennedy is assassinated (6); President Johnson plans the Great Society (8); Kennedy gets bills passed through Congress (4); Johnson is elected President (7); the Cuban Missile Crisis occurs (5).

Note-taking

Distribute the KWL chart on page 79 of this guide. Ask students to put what they know about John F. Kennedy in the **K** column and what they would like to know about John F. Kennedy in the **W** column of the chart. Have students share the information from their charts. As students read the chapter, have them complete the **L** column of their charts.

Assessing Content Knowledge

Ask students to respond to the following questions. You may wish to encourage students with higher language proficiency to help beginning level students understand the questions.

Beginning Level Questions

Encourage students at this level to think about the answers to these questions and offer short verbal responses.

1. Look at page 486. What was the New Frontier? (President Kennedy's ideas, goals, and programs for America)

2. Look at the map on page 488. Which candidate won the most states? (Nixon)

3. Look at the photo on page 491. Who are the three astronauts? (Neil Armstrong, Michael Collins, and Edwin Aldrin)

4. Look at page 493. What was the Berlin Wall? (a wall built by the East German government to keep people from leaving East Berlin)

5. Look at the graph on page 498. What is the difference in federal funding for education between 1960 and 1970? (approximately 2.4 billion)

Intermediate Level Questions

Encourage students at this level to offer verbal responses or short written responses to the following questions.

1. Look at Section 1. What was important about the TV debates of 1960? (It showed the power of television to influence elections.)

2. Look at Section 1. How did Americans feel about the space program? (Some supported it, and some did not.)

3. Look at Section 2. Why was the Bay of Pigs invasion unsuccessful? (The Cuban people attacked the exiles. More than 100 exiles were killed, and the rest were put in prison.)

4. Look at Section 2. What was the Cuban Missile Crisis? (The Soviet Union sent missiles to Cuba, and President Kennedy quarantined the country and said the United States would attack the Soviet Union if those missiles were used against the United States.)

5. Look at Section 3. What were the goals of the Great Society? (to help homeless people, older Americans, low-income people, and new immigrants)

Advanced Level Questions

Encourage students at this level to provide written responses in complete sentences to the following questions.

1. How did television help Kennedy win the presidential election? (He looked and sounded better than Nixon. People who watched the debates thought Kennedy had won them. Those who only heard them on radio thought they were even.)

2. What was the purpose of the programs that Kennedy started in the United States and in other countries? (The purpose of the programs was to help people.)

3. Why were some Americans unsupportive of the space program? (They felt the money should be spent to solve problems here on Earth.)

4. Why was the invasion of Cuba unwise? (It assumed that the Cuban people would rise up against Fidel Castro.)

5. What changes did President Johnson's program make in immigration laws? (The new immigration law in 1968 allowed more immigrants from Asia, Latin America, and Eastern Europe into the United States. In the past, immigration laws had favored Western Europeans.)

Closing the Chapter

Ask students to use the Sequence of Events chart that they completed for the Organizing Information activity on page 52 of this guide to write a summary about what they learned.

Chapter 27 Working for Change (1960–1975)

pages 504–521

▶ Introducing the Chapter

Tapping Prior Knowledge

Ask students to preview the chapter by reading the headings and subheadings and by looking at the art and photos (on pages 503, 504, 507, 508, 509, 513, and 517 of the Student Edition), the timeline (on pages 504–505 of the Student Edition), the numbered lists (on pages 508 and 513 of the Student Edition), and the map (on page 514 of the Student Edition). Then, direct students to the heading Rights for All Americans on page 516 of the Student Edition. Remind students that the United States is a country where people value freedom and individual rights. Ask students, *Why does inequality exist, and what is required to change it?*

Preteaching Vocabulary

Personalizing Vocabulary Begin by asking students to preview the chapter for five unfamiliar words or phrases and to record them in their Word Logs. Once students have identified these words and phrases, ask them to use their dictionaries to define them.

Identifying Essential Vocabulary Go over the pronunciation and meaning of each word and phrase in the box below. Then, provide sheets of graph paper with large boxes and ask students to use the words and phrases to create a crossword puzzle. Have students use sentences from the text as clues.

Word or Phrase	Meaning
rally	a gathering of people who believe in the same thing (p.507)
judged	decided if someone was right or wrong (p.508)
promoted	moved up (p.512)
ratify	to approve (p.514)
brutality	cruelty; unkindness (p.516)
unskilled job	work that does not require special abilities (p.517)
drain	to empty (p.518)

▶ Applying Content Knowledge

From the Chapter: Great Names in History (page 517)

Ask students to read Great Names in History: César Chávez on page 517 of the Student Edition. Distribute the KWL chart on page 79 of this guide. Ask students to put what they know about César Chávez in the **K** column and what they would like to know about César Chávez in the **W** column of the chart. Have students share the information from their charts. As students read the chapter, have them complete the **L** column of their charts. Remind students that César Chávez, like Martin Luther King, Jr., believed in nonviolence. Ask students, *Why is this a good way to protest?*

Organizing Information

Distribute the Idea Web on page 76 of this guide. As students read the chapter, ask them to fill in the Idea Web. Use the chapter title, **Working for Change**, as the central topic. Place the headings **African American Protests, Women Demand Equality,** and **Rights for All Americans** in the outer shapes. Then, ask students to list key details that they learned about each heading.

Note-taking

Ask students to read Section 3 entitled Rights for All Americans on pages 516–519 of the Student Edition. Then, distribute the four-column chart on page 70 of this guide. Have students label the columns **Name of Group, Conditions They Experienced, Goals of Their Movement,** and **Accomplishments.** Under the heading **Name of Group**, ask students to write **Chicanos, Puerto Ricans, Native Americans,** and **Asian Americans.** Have students use the information from Section 3 to complete their charts.

Assessing Content Knowledge

Ask students to respond to the following questions. You may wish to encourage students with higher language proficiency to help beginning level students understand the questions.

Beginning Level Questions

Encourage students at this level to think about the answers to these questions and offer short verbal responses.

1. Look at the photo on page 507. Who is the man in the picture? What did he believe? (Malcolm X; people should work together for freedom and equality)

2. Look at the photo on page 508. Who are the people in the picture, and what did they believe? (Black Panthers; believed in black pride and that black violence was the answer to white violence)

3. Look at page 513. What were five goals of the National Organization for Women? (See page 513.)

4. Look at page 516. Where did the largest Latino groups come from in the 1960s and 1970s? (Mexico, Puerto Rico, and Cuba)

5. Look at page 519. Who were the second-generation Japanese Americans, and what did they want from the U.S. government? (Nisei; wanted the U.S. government to pay the Japanese Americans who had been sent to internment camps during World War II)

Intermediate Level Questions

Encourage students at this level to offer verbal responses or short written responses to the following questions.

1. Look at Section 1. What did the Black Muslims believe? (that African Americans and white Americans should live separately)

2. Look at Section 1. Why was Malcolm X important? (He spoke out against separation.)

3. Look at Section 2. What movement was created by women's struggle for equal rights? (feminism)

4. Look at Section 3. Why did Mexican Americans use the word *Chicano* to describe themselves? (They felt it described the pride they felt in their culture.)

5. Look at Section 3. What were the two big problems on Native American reservations in the 1960s? (alcohol abuse and violence)

Advanced Level Questions

Encourage students at this level to provide written responses in complete sentences to the following questions.

1. Why did some African American groups think nonviolent protests were not working? (Change was happening too slowly.)

2. Why did the NAACP oppose black power? (It felt that black power would hurt the cause of equality.)

3. Why did riots break out in Watts? (An African American was arrested by a white police officer. African Americans were tired of discrimination.)

4. How did women further their cause for equality? (Answers will vary. Students should include that women lobbied Congress to pass legislation.)

5. Why were bilingual programs important to Mexican Americans? (Students could learn English and keep up with their regular schoolwork at the same time.)

Closing the Chapter

Ask students to use the Idea Web that they completed for the Organizing Information activity on page 54 of this guide to write a summary about what they learned in the chapter.

Chapter 28 The Vietnam War (1960–1973)

pages 522–541

▶ Introducing the Chapter

Tapping Prior Knowledge

Ask students to preview the chapter by reading the headings and subheadings and by looking at the art and photos (on pages 522, 528, 530, 531, 533, 535, 538, and 539 of the Student Edition), the timeline (on pages 522–523 of the Student Edition), the map (on page 527 of the Student Edition), and the chart (on page 532 of the Student Edition). Then, ask students to look at the picture on page 522 and work in small groups to answer the caption and share answers. Ask students, *Does this discussion help you to think about the Vietnam War?*

Preteaching Vocabulary

Personalizing Vocabulary Begin by asking students to preview the chapter for five unfamiliar words or phrases and to record them in their Word Logs. Once students have identified these words and phrases, ask them to use their dictionaries to define them.

Identifying Essential Vocabulary Go over the pronunciation and meaning of each word and phrase in the box below. Then, ask students to look at the word *controlled*. Explain that the word comes in many forms: *control, controls, controller,* and *controlling*. For example, *control* and *controls* can be verbs or nouns; *controller* is a noun; and *controlling* is an adjective. Tell students that the words *advisers, protests,* and *draft* also have many different forms.

Word or Phrase	Meaning
controlled	was in charge of (p.524)
adviser	someone who offers guidance and information (p.526)
took an important turn	something important happened (p.528)
however	but (p.528)
strayed	wandered (p.532)
antiwar protest	rally against the war (p.534)
draft card	a piece of paper that tells a person he has to go to war (p.534)

▶ Applying Content Knowledge

From the Chapter: Voices From the Past (page 530)

Ask students to read Voices From the Past: Protest Songs on page 530 of the Student Edition. Have students research other musicians and songs from this time period and share the message from one of the songs with the class. Ask students, *Why did people like Bob Dylan, Buffy Sainte Marie, Neil Young, and Phil Ochs protest the war by writing songs?*

Organizing Information

Distribute the Outline on page 75 of this guide. As students read the chapter, ask them to use the outline to fill in the headings and corresponding details.

> **Topic: The Vietnam War**
> I. A Distant War Divides a Nation
>   A.
>   B.
>   C.
> II. The Conflict Grows
>   A.
>   B.
>   C.
> III. The War Ends
>   A.
>   B.
>   C.

Using Manipulatives

Distribute index cards to students. Ask students to work in groups to write a label or draw a picture about an important event that occurred during the Vietnam War on one side of the index card and the date that the event took place on the other side of the index card. Collect each group's cards, shuffle them, and exchange them with another group's cards. Have the students in each group arrange the cards in the order in which the events took place without looking at the dates on the back of the cards. When students have finished arranging the cards, ask them to turn them over to see if they arrived at the correct sequence.

Assessing Content Knowledge

Ask students to respond to the following questions. You may wish to encourage students with higher language proficiency to help beginning level students understand the questions.

Beginning Level Questions

Encourage students at this level to think about the answers to these questions and offer short verbal responses.

1. Look at the timeline on pages 522–523. Who were the United States' Presidents during the Vietnam War? (Lyndon B. Johnson and Richard Nixon)

2. Look at the picture on page 528. Who is this man, and what is he saying? (President Lyndon B. Johnson; telling Americans about the attack on a U.S. warship in the Gulf of Tonkin near North Vietnam)

3. Look at the chart on page 532. What were six weaknesses of the American forces in Vietnam? (See page 532.)

4. Look at page 537. What was Vietnamization? (a plan for turning over the fighting of the Vietnam War to the South Vietnamese)

5. Look at page 539. What is the Vietnam Veterans Memorial? (a memorial to all the men and women killed and missing as a result of the Vietnam War)

Intermediate Level Questions

Encourage students at this level to offer verbal responses or short written responses to the following questions.

1. Look at Section 1. Who was Ho Chi Minh? (the leader of the war for independence in Vietnam)

2. Look at Section 1. How did the Viet Cong affect the Vietnam War? (When the Viet Cong joined the North Vietnamese army to fight Diem's forces, it marked the beginning of the Vietnam War.)

3. Look at Section 2. What two weapons did United States forces drop from planes during the Vietnam War? (napalm bombs and Agent Orange)

4. Look at Section 2. Why were the Viet Cong forces stronger than the American forces? (See page 532.)

5. Look at Section 3. What did the Pentagon Papers show? (that the United States was planning to enter the war even though President Johnson promised not to)

Advanced Level Questions

Encourage students at this level to provide written responses in complete sentences to the following questions.

1. Why did Vietnam fight a war against France? (Vietnam fought a war against France to gain its independence.)

2. Why did President Johnson believe that the United States had to get involved in the Vietnam War? (A U.S. warship was attacked by the North Vietnamese, and Johnson believed that the United States had to fight back.)

3. How did the Tet offensive affect the American people? (Americans found out how bad the war really was, and fewer people supported it.)

4. Why did President Nixon bomb the Ho Chi Minh trail? (Nixon believed that bombing the Ho Chi Minh trail would stop the North Vietnamese from sending troops and supplies to the Viet Cong in the South.)

5. Why did veterans of the Vietnam War feel as if they were not treated the same way veterans from other wars had been treated? (Many veterans felt that Americans who protested the war did not respect the sacrifices they had made.)

Closing the Chapter

Ask students to use the Outline they completed for the Organizing Information activity on page 56 of this guide to write a summary about what they learned in the chapter.

Chapter 29

Entering a New Decade (1970–1975)

pages 542–557

Introducing the Chapter

Tapping Prior Knowledge

Ask students to preview the chapter by reading the headings and subheadings and by looking at the art and photos (on pages 542, 545, 549, 551, and 553 of the Student Edition), the timeline (on pages 542–543 of the Student Edition), and the numbered list (on page 548 of the Student Edition). Then, tell students to study the timeline on pages 542–543 entitled A Difficult Decade. Ask students to draw on their own experience and what they learned in previous chapters to decide which of those events were good for the United States and which were not. As part of the discussion, suggest that students explain their decisions. After the discussion, ask students, *Does this discussion help you to understand why this was such a difficult period in the United States?*

Preteaching Vocabulary

Personalizing Vocabulary Begin by asking students to preview the chapter for five unfamiliar words or phrases and to record them in their Word Logs. Once students have identified these words and phrases, ask them to use their dictionaries to define them.

Identifying Essential Vocabulary Go over the pronunciation and meaning of each word and phrase in the box below. Then, provide sheets of graph paper with large boxes and ask students to use the words and phrases to create a crossword puzzle. Have students use sentences from the text as clues.

Word or Phrase	Meaning
decade	ten years (p.543)
hinted	gave a small sign (p.544)
hand over	give (p.554)
to give up	to let go of (p.554)
granted a pardon	gave a person freedom from punishment (p.555)

Applying Content Knowledge

From the Chapter: Connecting History and Economics (page 551)

Ask students to read Connecting History and Economics: Inflation on page 551 of the Student Edition. Then, distribute the three-column chart on page 74 of this guide. Ask students to write the headings **Category**, _____ **Years Ago**, and _____ **Years Ago** for the three columns. Ask students to work in groups to complete the chart by researching costs in their town/city or state for each of the following categories: *housing, cars, gasoline, hamburgers,* and *movies.* Students should search for prices/costs for two of the following time spans: 50 years ago, 20 years ago, 10 years ago, 5 years ago, or 2 years ago. Ask students to write their conclusions regarding inflation over the past 50 years.

Costs in My Town/City or State		
Category	_____ Years Ago	_____ Years Ago
Housing		
Cars		
Gasoline		
Hamburgers		
Movies		

Organizing Information

Distribute the Outline on page 75 of this guide. As students read the chapter, ask them to use the outline to fill in the headings and corresponding details.

Note-taking

Distribute the Sequence of Events chart on page 71 of this guide. Ask students to review Section 3 entitled Watergate. Then, have students use the Sequence of Events chart to write the steps that led to the resignation of President Nixon.

Assessing Content Knowledge

Ask students to respond to the following questions. You may wish to encourage students with higher language proficiency to help beginning level students understand the questions.

Beginning Level Questions

Encourage students at this level to think about the answers to these questions and offer short verbal responses.

1. Look at page 544. Who was the first American President to visit China while in office? (Nixon)

2. Look at page 545. What did the United States do in Chile? (It fought Allende's government.)

3. Look at page 549. How was the Vietnam War causing problems for the U.S. economy? (The government was borrowing money to pay for the war.)

4. Look at page 553. Who are Bob Woodward and Carl Bernstein? (reporters for the *Washington Post* who uncovered the truth in the Watergate scandal)

5. Look at page 555. What did the tapes prove about President Nixon and Watergate? (President Nixon knew about the cover-up and helped plan it.)

Intermediate Level Questions

Encourage students at this level to offer verbal responses or short written responses to the following questions.

1. Look at Section 1. What was President Nixon's agreement with the Soviet leader? (to limit the number of new weapons each would build and to sell grain to the Soviet Union)

2. Look at Section 1. Why did the United States help to overthrow Allende in Chile? (He followed Communist ideas.)

3. Look at Section 2. What were two problems with the U.S. economy while Nixon was in office? (Unemployment rose, and there was inflation.)

4. Look at Section 3. Why do you think President Nixon covered up his involvement in Watergate? (Answers will vary. Students' answers might include the issues of legality, of embarrassment, or a belief that it actually could be covered up.)

5. Look at Section 3. What was the Watergate scandal? (The Watergate group had been paid with Republican campaign money to break into the Watergate.)

Advanced Level Questions

Encourage students at this level to provide written responses in complete sentences to the following questions.

1. How did normalizing relations with China help the United States? (It started the end of the Cold War and led to better relations with the Soviets.)

2. Why do you think the United States supported dictators over an elected leader? (Answers will vary. Students' answers might include fear of communism, ability to influence dictators, or supporting rebels.)

3. What was Nixon's plan to shift control of programs to the states? (He used revenue sharing and sent federal money to the states to spend as they wished.)

4. How did the U.S. support of Israel add to the problems in the economy? (The Arab states in the Middle East were angry, so they banned oil shipments to the United States and created a gasoline shortage, which increased the cost of travel, food, and heating, and added to inflation.)

5. Why do you think President Ford granted a pardon to Richard Nixon? (Answers will vary. Students' answers might include a need to put an end to the scandal; to end the embarrassment for everyone; to support the Republican party; believing that the disgrace of resignation was enough.)

Closing the Chapter

Ask students to use the Outline they completed for the Organizing Information activity on page 58 of this guide to summarize what they learned in the chapter.

Chapter 30

Changes at Home and Abroad (1976–1988)

pages 560–577

▶ Introducing the Chapter

Tapping Prior Knowledge

Ask students to preview the chapter by reading the headings and subheadings and by looking at the art and photos (on pages 559, 560, 562, 565, 568, 570, and 575 of the Student Edition), the timeline (on pages 560–561 of the Student Edition), and the chart (on page 573 of the Student Edition). Brainstorm with students to create a list of qualities they admire in people. Discuss the qualities with students. Then, ask them to select the qualities from the list that they believe a successful leader must have. Then, direct students to the photograph of President Carter on page 560 of the Student Edition and President Reagan on page 568 of the Student Edition. Remind students that these were two very different kinds of leaders. Ask students, *What kinds of qualities should world leaders today have in order to succeed?*

Preteaching Vocabulary

Personalizing Vocabulary Begin by asking students to preview the chapter for five unfamiliar words or phrases and to record them in their Word Logs. Once students have identified these words and phrases, ask them to use their dictionaries to define them.

Identifying Essential Vocabulary Go over the pronunciation and meaning of each word and phrase in the box below. Then, ask students to write a paragraph using as many of the words and phrases as they can. Students may wish to consult their bilingual dictionaries.

Word or Phrase	Meaning
outsider	stranger (p.562)
held captive	be a prisoner (p.565)
let go	release; free (p.565)
recession	when people buy less (p.568)
joblessness	no work (p.568)
outlawed	not legal; not allowed (p.574)

▶ Applying Content Knowledge

From the Chapter: Citizenship Link (page 570)

Ask students to read Citizenship Link: Geraldine Ferraro on page 570 of the Student Edition. Explain to students that Geraldine Ferraro was the first woman from one of the major political parties to run for Vice President of the United States. Ask students to research on the Internet or in their school library what it means to be Vice President. Ask students, *What kinds of responsibilities does a Vice President have?* Ask students to summarize their research in a paragraph.

Organizing Information

Tell students that President Carter and President Reagan's decisions made many people happy and many people unhappy. Ask students to work in small groups to make a list of four decisions made by each President and the people or groups who liked and disliked those decisions. You might wish to ask students to compare their lists with another group after they have finished.

Note-taking

Distribute the Outline on page 75 of this guide. Ask students to take notes on either the Iranian hostage crisis or the Iran-Contra affair. Then, have students use only their notes to retell one of those events to a partner.

Personalizing the Lesson

Ask students to work in a small group to discuss this question: *Should the United States get involved in the affairs of other countries?* Ask each group to choose a representative to report on the group's conclusions.

Assessing Content Knowledge

Ask students to respond to the following questions. You may wish to encourage students with higher language proficiency to help beginning level students understand the questions.

Beginning Level Questions

Encourage students at this level to think about the answers to these questions and offer short verbal responses.

1. Look at the photo on page 560. Who are the three world leaders? (Carter, Sadat, and Begin)

2. Look at page 564. What did President Carter do to punish the Soviets for invading Afghanistan? (He put an embargo on U.S. grain and refused to allow U.S. athletes to participate in the summer Olympics.)

3. Look at page 565. Why did followers of the Ayatollah take about 50 Americans as hostages? (They were angry that the United States had helped the shah.)

4. Look at page 569. Who were the groups in the New Right who helped Reagan win the election? (business groups and religious groups)

5. Look at page 575. How did Mikhail Gorbachev change the Soviet Union? (glasnost, met with Reagan, signed a treaty, withdrew troops from Afghanistan)

Intermediate Level Questions

Encourage students at this level to offer verbal responses or short written responses to the following questions.

1. Look at Section 1. What were two new departments of government that President Carter created? (Department of Education; Department of Energy)

2. Look at Section 1. Why did President Carter announce that the United States would not be allowed to participate in the Olympics? (because the Soviet Union invaded Afghanistan)

3. Look at Section 1. What did the Camp David Accords say that Egypt would do? (enter into peaceful relations and trade with Israel)

4. Look at Section 2. How did President Reagan view government? (It should be small and make few rules.)

5. Look at Section 3. How did the Iran-Contra affair hurt President Reagan's reputation? (The special prosecutor found that his advisers had broken the law.)

Advanced Level Questions

Encourage students at this level to provide written responses in complete sentences to the following questions.

1. Why do you think it was so important to Americans when Jimmy Carter said he would never lie to them? (Answers will vary. Students' answers might include the recent scandal with Nixon and a strong need of people to feel that they can trust their leaders.)

2. What were two problems President Carter could not solve during his term as President? (Problems that President Carter could not solve included inflation, joblessness, relations with the Soviet Union, and the Iranian hostage crisis.)

3. What programs were hurt during President Reagan's administration? (Education and social programs were hurt during President Reagan's administration.)

4. How did President Reagan help the economy? (His programs reduced inflation and joblessness.)

5. What did President Reagan do in Nicaragua? In El Salvador? (In Nicaragua, the United States gave weapons to the rebels and blockaded ports to stop supplies for the Sandinistas that came from the Soviets and Cuba. In El Salvador, the United States helped the government by training special groups of soldiers from El Salvador who kidnapped and killed suspected Communist rebels.)

Closing the Chapter

Ask students to use the headings and the subheadings to create a list of questions about the chapter. For example, the heading A New Kind of Leader could become the question *Who was known as a new kind of leader? Why?* and the subheading Successes and Problems at Home could become the questions *What were some successes at home? What were some problems at home?* Ask students to answer each of these questions and use their answers to write a summary about what they learned.

Chapter 31 / Progress and Problems (1988–2000)

pages 578–597

▶ Introducing the Chapter

Tapping Prior Knowledge

Ask students to preview the chapter by reading the headings and subheadings and by looking at the art and photos (on pages 578, 580, 581, 582, 585, 588, 593, 594, and 595 of the Student Edition), the timeline (on pages 578–579 of the Student Edition), the map (on page 587 of the Student Edition), and the chart (on page 589 of the Student Edition). Then, ask students if they can think of examples in which a change or improvement in one part of their lives created more problems for them to solve. Ask students, *How can progress in the world also raise new problems that need to be solved?*

Preteaching Vocabulary

Personalizing Vocabulary Begin by asking students to preview the chapter for five unfamiliar words or phrases and to record them in their Word Logs. Once students have identified these words and phrases, ask them to use their dictionaries to define them.

Identifying Essential Vocabulary Go over the pronunciation and meaning of each word and phrase in the box below. Then, distribute the Spider Web on page 73 of this guide and ask students to decide which phrases in the box below are about politics, economics, or war. Ask students to label the spokes of their webs **Politics, Economics,** and **War** and to fill in their webs with phrases from the box below.

Word or Phrase	Meaning
federal budget deficit	a shortage of government money (p.581)
national debt	money that the country owes (p.581)
third-party candidate	not a Democrat or a Republican (p.581)
forcibly removed	to take away with power (p.585)
all necessary means	everyway possible (p.586)
cut back on	use less (p.591)
welfare system	a program that gives money to people who need it to live (p.593)

▶ Applying Content Knowledge

From the Chapter: Voices From the Past (page 595)

Ask students to read Voices From the Past: Maya Angelou on page 595 of the Student Edition. You might wish to read the section of poetry aloud to students. Ask students to choose their favorite line from the poem. Ask students, *Why did you choose that line from the poem?* Then, have students choose a word or phrase from the line they chose and ask them to write their own poem using that word or phrase.

Summarizing

Distribute the Who, What, Why, Where, When, and How chart on page 81 of this guide. Have students work with a partner to write six questions (who, what, why, where, when, and how) about Colin Powell. Then, ask students to read Great Names in History: Colin Powell on page 588 of the Student Edition and write answers to their questions. After students write the answers to their questions, have them write a paragraph that summarizes what they learned about Colin Powell.

Organizing Information

Distribute the Outline on page 75 of this guide. As students read the chapter, ask them to use the outline to fill in the headings and corresponding details.

Personalizing the Lesson

Ask students to look at the Conflict and Change Around the World, 1983–1994, chart on page 589 of the Student Edition. Remind students that the United States and the United Nations are involved in many ways all over the world—troops, peacekeeping forces, restrictions, and diplomacy. Ask students to think of a conflict that is happening in the world today. Then, ask students, *What method do you suppose would be the best way to solve the problem?* Have students write a paragraph that states the problem they chose and explains their reasons for the method they selected.

Assessing Content Knowledge

Ask students to respond to the following questions. You may wish to encourage students with higher language proficiency to help beginning level students understand the questions.

Beginning Level Questions

Encourage students at this level to think about the answers to these questions and offer short verbal responses.

1. Look at the picture on page 578. What is happening in the photograph? (The Berlin Wall has come down, and people are celebrating.)

2. Look at page 582. What were three of President Clinton's accomplishments? (The economy improved; joblessness fell; inflation stayed low; and there was a budget surplus.)

3. Look at the map on page 587. Which countries experienced Iraqi missile strikes? (Israel, Lebanon, Kuwait, Saudi Arabia, and Bahrain)

4. Look at the chart on page 589. What information does the last column give? (the U.S. action that answered the problem in the second column)

5. Look at pages 592–593. What are three new programs that changed the lives of Americans in the 1990s? (Americans with Disabilities Act [ADA]; Welfare Reform; and Health Care Reform)

Intermediate Level Questions

Encourage students at this level to offer verbal responses or short written responses to the following questions.

1. Look at Section 1. Why did President Bush raise taxes even though he had promised that he would not? (The federal budget deficits were a big problem.)

2. Look at Section 1. What is the role of the Senate in the impeachment process? (to conduct the trial)

3. Look at Section 2. What did the Serbs do in Bosnia and Kosovo? (forcibly removed Bosnians and Albanians from their countries)

4. Look at Section 2. What did President Bush do when Iraq invaded Kuwait? (He went to the United Nations, and he formed a coalition of nations.)

5. Look at Section 3. Why did President Clinton believe that health care reform was important? (because millions of people did not have health insurance)

Advanced Level Questions

Encourage students at this level to provide written responses in complete sentences to the following questions.

1. Why was President Clinton a popular President? (He could make people feel that he cared about them.)

2. Why was President Clinton impeached by the House of Representatives? (He was accused of lying to a grand jury.)

3. Why did many Russians have a difficult time after the fall of communism? (Many Russians were used to being controlled by Communists for a long time.)

4. What was the purpose of Operation Desert Storm? (The purpose of Desert Storm was to force Iraq to leave Kuwait and to remove Iraq as a threat in the Middle East.)

5. Why was passing the Brady Bill important? (The bill required a waiting period and background checks for gun buyers, which could help to prevent future gun-related incidents.)

Closing the Chapter

Ask students to use the Outline they completed for the Organizing Information activity on page 62 of this guide to summarize what they learned in the chapter.

Chapter 32

A New Century (1990–the future)

pages 598–611

▶ Introducing the Chapter

Tapping Prior Knowledge

Ask students to preview the chapter by reading the headings and subheadings and by looking at the art and photos (on pages 598, 600, 601, 602, 603, 604, 607, and 608 of the Student Edition) and the timeline (on pages 598–599 of the Student Edition). Ask students to describe the events that are covered in this chapter. Students should understand that the chapter discusses the challenges the United States faced at the end of the twentieth century and the beginning of the twenty-first century. Have students brainstorm challenges that they face today. Ask students, *Does this discussion help you understand how other people living in the United States are affected by world events?*

Preteaching Vocabulary

Personalizing Vocabulary Begin by asking students to preview the chapter for five unfamiliar words or phrases and to record them in their Word Logs. Once students have identified these words and phrases, ask them to use their dictionaries to define them.

Identifying Essential Vocabulary Go over the pronunciation and meaning of each phrase in the box below. Then, distribute an index card to each student. Ask each student to write a question on the index card using one of the phrases. Then, have students select a partner to exchange cards with and have each student answer their partner's question.

Word or Phrase	Meaning
legal battle	an argument or disagreement that is fought in a court of law (p.601)
driven from power	removed from power (p.603)
coalition of countries	a temporary alliance of countries for a purpose (p.603)
spray cans	containers that produce drops of the liquid inside (p.607)
cut down on	decrease (p.607)

▶ Applying Content Knowledge

From the Chapter: A Closer Look (page 602)

Ask students to read A Closer Look: The Heroes of September 11, 2001, on page 602 of the Student Edition. Explain to students that many groups of people from around the United States acted bravely during and after the terrorist attacks of **September 11, 2001**. Distribute the two-column chart on page 68 of this guide. Ask students to label the topic **September 11, 2001**, and the columns **Groups That Acted Bravely** and **Their Actions**. Have students work in groups to complete their charts using information from A Closer Look: The Heroes of September 11, 2001. You may wish to have students use their charts to write a paragraph about the brave actions of the heroes.

Using Visuals

Ask students to look at the photo of the millennium celebration on page 598 of the Student Edition. Ask students, *What are other ways in which people celebrate the coming of a new year or new century?* Students' answers might include small family celebrations, making new-year's resolutions, and setting goals for the new year. Write students' suggestions on the chalkboard. Then, ask students to record the list of suggestions and use the list to ask students in other classes what their favorite ways to celebrate a new year are. When students finish polling their peers, they can create a bar graph that shows their results.

Using Manipulatives

Ask students to work in groups to choose one environmental issue to research and then illustrate on posterboard. Students might wish to create large floor-to-ceiling posters to allow space for drawings, pictures, and text. You might wish to suggest that students also consider possible solutions to the environmental problem as part of their display.

Personalizing the Lesson

Have students work in groups and ask them, *What are five things that people can do to ensure a better future for the world?*

Assessing Content Knowledge

Ask students to respond to the following questions. You may wish to encourage students with higher language proficiency to help beginning level students understand the questions.

Beginning Level Questions

Encourage students at this level to think about the answers to these questions and offer short verbal responses.

1. Look at the photo on page 600. Who was elected President in 2000? (George W. Bush)

2. Look at the photo on page 602. Who are these people? (rescue teams)

3. Look at page 603. Where were U.S. soldiers sent during Operation Enduring Freedom? (Afghanistan)

4. Look at page 607. How does recycling help the environment? (Recycling reduces the amount of waste.)

5. Look at page 608. What does ISS stand for? (International Space Station)

Intermediate Level Questions

Encourage students at this level to offer verbal responses or short written responses to the following questions.

1. Look at Section 1. What is the difference between popular votes and electoral votes? (Popular votes are votes cast by citizens in a presidential election. Electoral votes are votes cast by chosen electors in a presidential election.)

2. Look at Section 1. What are three examples of foreign terrorist attacks on U.S. interests after 1993? (the bombing of U.S. embassy buildings in Kenya and Tanzania, the attack of the USS *Cole* in Yemen, and the attacks of September 11, 2001)

3. Look at Section 1. What were two U.S. military operations in the war on terrorism? (Operation Enduring Freedom in Afghanistan and Operation Iraqi Freedom in Iraq)

4. Look at Section 2. What are two environmental concerns? (Possible answers include two of the following: acid rain, global warming, holes in the ozone layer, and not enough places to put garbage.)

5. Look at Section 2. What are nonrenewable resources? (resources that will run out one day and cannot be replaced, like oil and coal)

Advanced Level Questions

Encourage students at this level to provide written responses in complete sentences to the following questions.

1. What was the relationship between the Taliban government in Afghanistan and Osama bin Laden? (The Taliban government protected Osama bin Laden and the al Qaeda group of terrorists.)

2. What was the role of the UN in Iraq? (The UN passed a resolution demanding that Iraq destroy all of its deadly weapons and sent weapons inspectors to Iraq to make sure the weapons were destroyed.)

3. Why should the United States rely more on renewable resources of energy? (They can be replaced by nature and do not pollute the environment.)

4. What is the purpose of the International Space Station? (Astronauts from many nations work together to conduct experiments and develop technologies for the future.)

5. Why is being a country of invention and change an advantage? (Answers will vary.)

Closing the Chapter

Ask students to use the headings and the subheadings to create a list of questions about the chapter. For example, the heading Protecting Americans at Home could become the question *How did the U.S. government protect Americans at home?* and the heading Using Energy Wisely could become the question *How can Americans use energy wisely?* Ask students to answer each of these questions and use their answers to write a summary about what they learned.

About the Graphic Organizers

Graphic organizers are valuable tools for ESL/ELL students. They show patterns and relationships that support language acquisition and that help students access academic content, consolidate their thinking, and help them to generate new ideas. For example, the Who, What, Why, Where, When, and How chart gives students an opportunity to use adverbs to write *wh-* questions as a method for accessing content.

The graphic organizers and visuals provided here can be used in a variety of ways. They can be made into overhead slides and used for visual instruction or for group work. The pages can also be reproduced for use by students. All of the graphic organizers correlate to an activity in this guide. Students can use them to complete their activities, adding to them as needed. Below is a description of each graphic organizer and visual with suggestions for their use. Each of these graphic organizers can also be downloaded from www.esl-ell.com.

Two-column Chart (page 68)
This graphic organizer can be used for many purposes. The columns can be labeled as needed. Then relevant information is written in each cell of the chart.

World Map (page 69)
This map allows students to see all the continents at once. It can be used for labeling and identifying activities.

Four-column Chart (page 70)
This graphic organizer can be used for many purposes. The columns can be labeled as needed. Then relevant information is written in each cell of the chart.

Sequence of Events Chart (page 71)
This graphic organizer is a flowchart to help students sort information chronologically. You may wish to have students use this graphic organizer when making to-do lists and writing out directions. Students might also use the Sequence of Events chart to plan out role-playing activities or while writing conversations.

Timeline (page 72)
This graphic organizer is used to organize a series of events

Spider Web (page 73)
This graphic organizer is used to organize several levels of elaboration. The main topic is written in the center circle. Attributes are listed on the spokes. Specific details are listed on the horizontal lines extending from each spoke. This organizer can also be used to determine main ideas and supporting details. You may also want students to use a Spider Web when brainstorming ideas.

Three-column Chart (page 74)
This graphic organizer can be used for many purposes. The columns can be labeled as needed. Then relevant information is written in each cell of the chart.

Outline (page 75)
This graphic organizer is used to help students organize and write outlines. An outline can be used to organize fully developed ideas into paragraphs in which supporting details are given. For activities that require longer outlines, outlines can be extended by continuing the numbering on the back of the reproducible page.

Idea Web (page 76)
This graphic organizer is used to cluster supporting details around a central topic. It is very useful for brainstorming. The main concept or idea is written in the center shape. Related ideas are listed in the outer shapes.

Venn Diagram (page 77)
This graphic organizer is used to compare and contrast things or ideas. Each circle should be labeled as one of the two things being contrasted. Then the differences are written in the outer section of each circle. The similarities are written in the section in which the circles overlap.

Main Idea and Supporting Details Chart (page 78)

This graphic organizer is used to identify supporting details that relate to a central topic. The main idea is written in the first box. Supporting details are in the boxes labeled Supporting Details. Students can use the main idea and supporting details to write a paragraph for the box labeled Summary.

KWL Chart (page 79)

This chart can be used before and after each chapter in the Student Edition. The KWL chart is used to help students access their knowledge of a topic and to add to what they already know. KWL stands for "Know," "Want To Know," and "Learned."

Cause and Effect Chart (page 80)

This graphic organizer helps students organize the effects of a particular cause. Students write the cause in the top oval and the effects in the remaining ovals.

Who, What, Why, Where, When, and How Chart (page 81)

This graphic organizer is used to help students identify important information while they read. Students complete the chart by answering the questions as they read. This chart can be used to help students understand textbook chapters or news articles they read.

Individual Activity Rubric (page 82)

The Individual Activity Rubric can be customized for different activities. The first eight criteria in the rubric are generic. The last two criteria are left blank. These criteria should be based on specific tasks required and filled in by the teacher. You may wish to distribute a rubric to students as a guide for completing an activity or as a self-assessment tool.

Group Activity Rubric (page 83)

The Group Activity Rubric can be customized for different activities. The first eight criteria in the rubric are generic. The last two criteria are left blank. These criteria should be based on specific tasks required and filled in by the teacher. You may wish to distribute a rubric to students as a guide for completing a group activity or as a self-assessment tool for a student who worked in a group.

Chapter Goals and Self-assessment (page 84)

This reproducible can be used for goal-setting and self-assessment. When starting a chapter, have students write the chapter Learning Objectives onto this worksheet. At the end of the chapter, students can "self-check" their understanding by writing about it. They can also record the date when they completed all their objectives.

Name _____ Date _____

Two-column Chart

Topic: _____

Name _____ Date _____

World Map

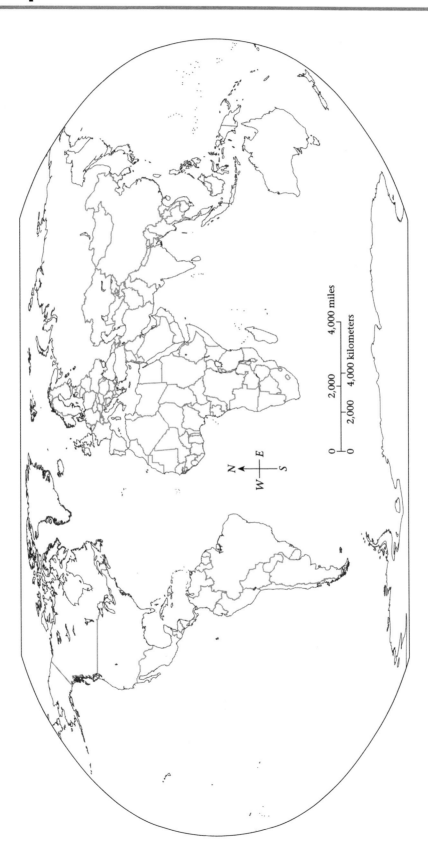

Name _____ Date _____

Four-column Chart

Topic: _____

Name _____ Date _____

Sequence of Events Chart

TOPIC

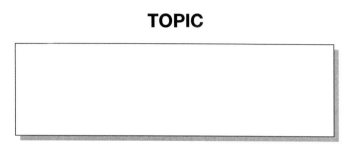

SEQUENCE OF EVENTS

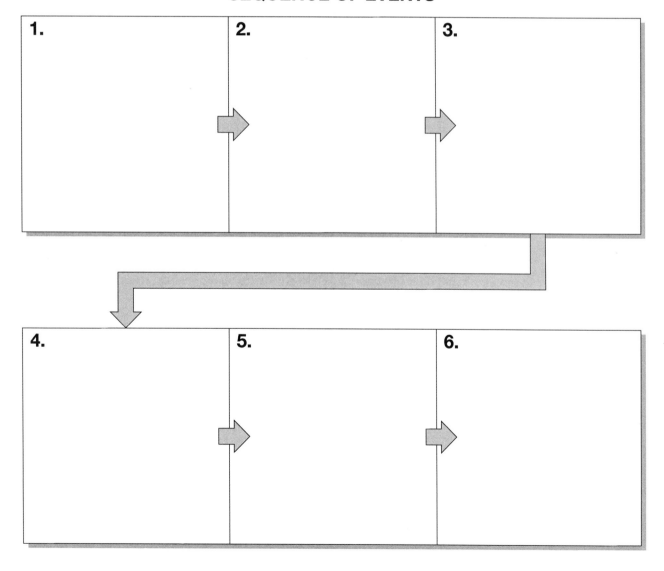

Name _____ Date _____

Timeline

Name _____ Date _____

Spider Web

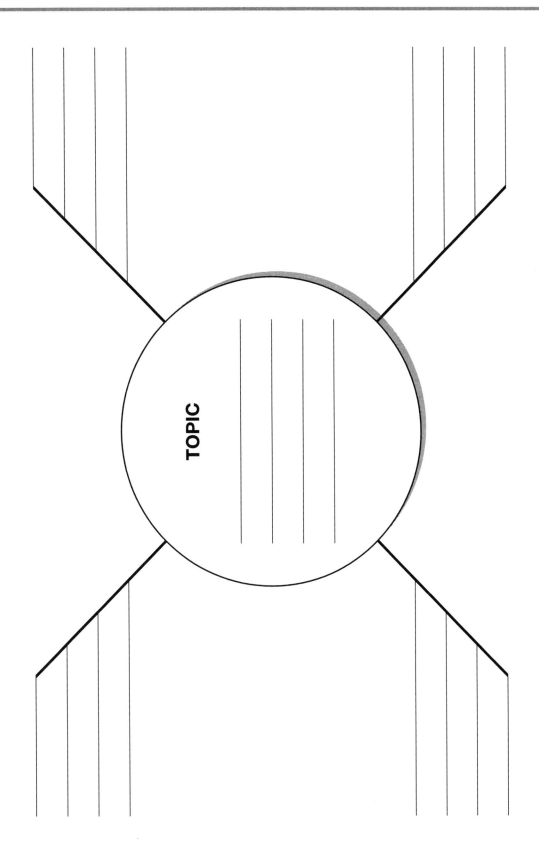

TOPIC

Name _____ Date _____

Three-column Chart

Topic: _____

Name _____ Date _____

Outline

Topic: _____

I. [_____]

    A. _____

       1. _____

       2. _____

    B. _____

       1. _____

       2. _____

    C. _____

       1. _____

       2. _____

II. [_____]

    A. _____

       1. _____

       2. _____

    B. _____

       1. _____

       2. _____

    C. _____

       1. _____

       2. _____

Name _____ Date _____

Idea Web

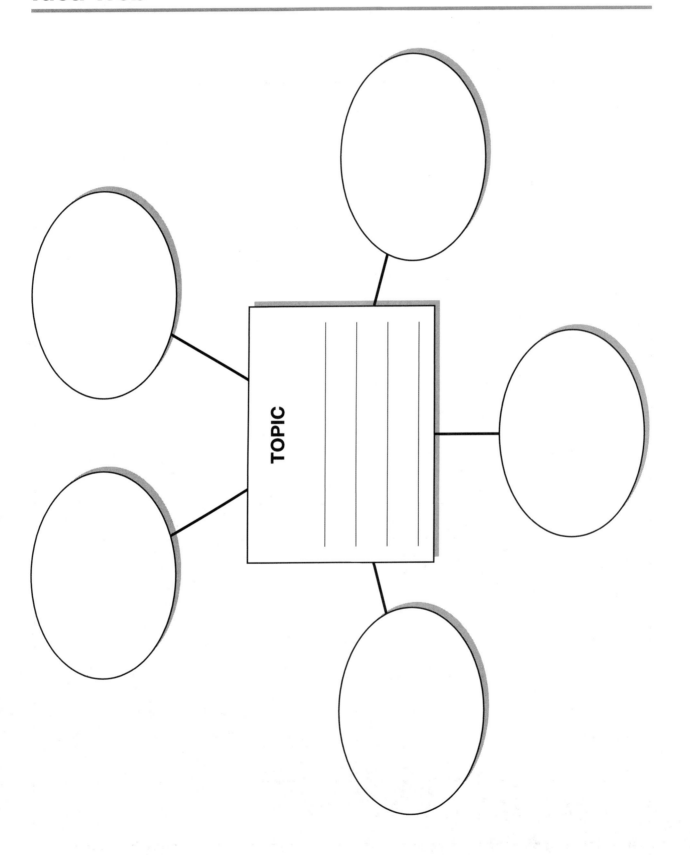

Name _____ Date _____

Venn Diagram

Topic: _____

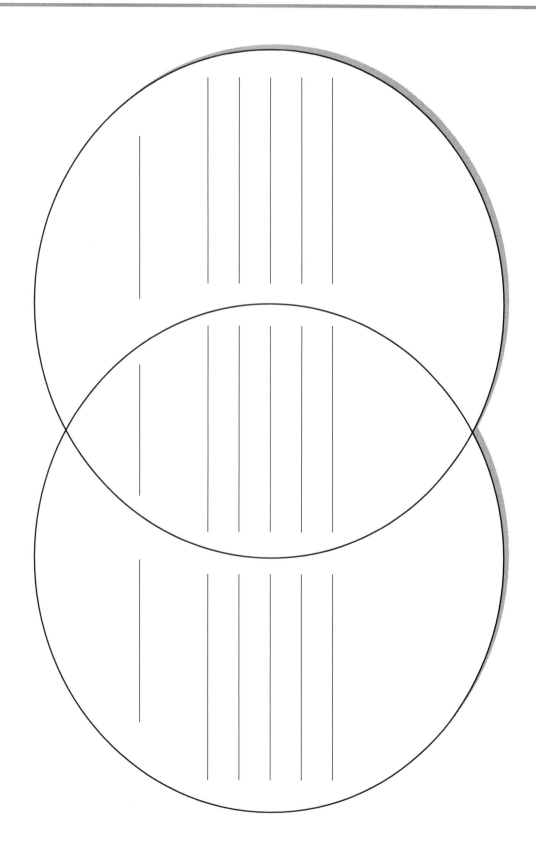

Name _____ Date _____

Main Idea and Supporting Details Chart

MAIN IDEA

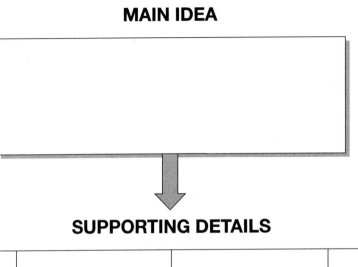

SUPPORTING DETAILS

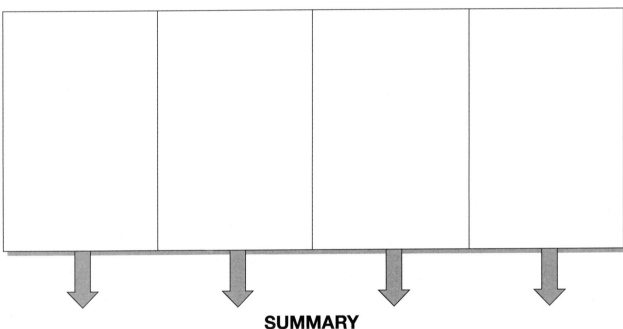

SUMMARY

Name _____ Date _____

KWL Chart

K (What I Know)	W (What I Want to Know)	L (What I Have Learned)

Name _____ Date _____

Cause and Effect Chart

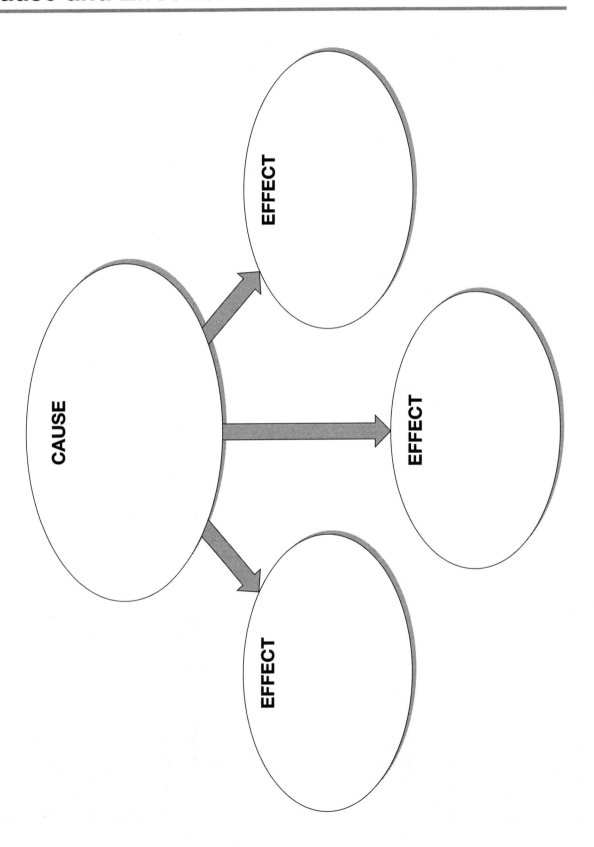

Name _____ Date _____

Who, What, Why, Where, When, and How Chart

WHO	
WHAT	
WHY	
WHERE	
WHEN	
HOW	

Individual Activity Rubric

Name ———————————————— Date ——————————

Chapter Number ————— Activity ——————————————

Directions

Check ✓ one box in a column to finish each sentence.

Give each check ✓ the assigned number of points.

Add the points in each column. Write the sum. Then add across to find the total score.

You may wish to add two criteria of your own to the rubric.

POINTS	10	9	8	7	6
For this activity, Student's name ———	all of the time	most of the time	half of the time	less than half of the time	none of the time
followed directions					
asked questions when help was needed					
worked independently when required					
used appropriate resources and materials					
completed assigned tasks					
showed an understanding of the content					
presented materials without errors					
explained thinking with support					
——————					
——————					
POINTS	+	+	+	+	=

TOTAL SCORE

Group Activity Rubric

Name _____ Date _____

Chapter Number _____ Activity _____

Directions
Check ✓ one box in a column to finish each sentence.
Give each check ✓ the assigned number of points.
Add the points in each column. Write the sum. Then add across to find the total score.
You may wish to add two criteria of your own to the rubric.

POINTS	10	9	8	7	6
For this activity, Student's name _____	all of the time	most of the time	half of the time	less than half of the time	none of the time
followed directions					
asked questions when help was needed					
worked independently when required					
used appropriate resources and materials					
completed assigned tasks					
showed an understanding of the content					
presented materials without errors					
explained thinking with support					
_____					
_____					
POINTS	+	+	+	+	=

TOTAL SCORE

Chapter Goals and Self-assessment

Name _____ Date _____

Chapter Title _____ Pages _____

Write each Learning Objective on a line below.

Did I understand it?

	Yes	No
• _____	❏	❏
• _____	❏	❏
• _____	❏	❏
• _____	❏	❏
• _____	❏	❏
• _____	❏	❏

Complete each statement.

This chapter is about _____

_____

An important person or event from this chapter is _____

_____

I learned a writing skill. It is _____

_____

I completed Chapter _____ entitled _____

_____ and all of my Learning Objectives on

_____ .